THE TEEN
MONEY
MANUAL

A Guide to Cash, Credit, Spending, Saving, Work, Wealth, and More

by KARA McGUIRE

Award-winning personal
finance writer, researcher,
and public speaker

CAPSTONE YOUNG READERS
a capstone imprint

EARNING

SAVING

TABLE OF CONTENTS

LET'S MAKE SOME MONEY!

Everyone loves payday—from the first quarter you earned for setting the table to the weekly allowance you squirreled away to buy toys or iPhone apps. Then comes the day of that first official paycheck and all of the responsibility that goes along with it.

That includes spending wisely and saving for the future. It means making smart decisions but still having fun. Learn all about the ins and outs of making money—from paychecks to paying taxes, finding jobs, and starting businesses. And best of all, learn how to earn money without lifting a finger.

CHAPTER ONE

JOBS AND CAREER PLANNING

It's common for teens to juggle schoolwork and paid work, whether it's the occasional babysitting job or waiting tables 20 hours a week at a restaurant. Teens need money for hanging out, for hobbies, or for gas for the car. Then there is the cost of big things, such as saving for a car, helping with college tuition, or taking an overseas trip with the school orchestra. It's understandable why sometimes earning money seems more important than keeping up grades or working on college applications.

EDUCATION AND EARNINGS

Your number one job as a teen is to get good grades, gain experiences from school and community activities, and prepare for higher education. Your education affects job opportunities and how much you will be able to earn. The lifetime median earnings of a worker with just a high school diploma is $1.3 million. It may sound like a ton of money today, but it averages to $15 per hour—that's not much once you consider daily expenses and how long you could live. Americans with a bachelor's degree can plan on median lifetime earnings of $2.3 million. Those who stay in school for a doctoral or professional degree, such as medicine or law, earn a median of $3.6 million.

Although there are certainly exceptions to this rule, having a college degree increases your chances of earning more money and opens more doors to interesting, fulfilling careers. As the chart indicates, nearly 80 percent of people with bachelor's degrees or higher earn $200,000 a year or more. Less than 10 percent of people with a high school education earn a similar amount.

If a four-year college is not in your plans, some people—such as electricians, construction managers, and sales managers—have average lifetime earnings that come close to the earnings of workers with bachelor's degrees.

WELL-EDUCATED AMERICANS HAVE HIGH INCOMES

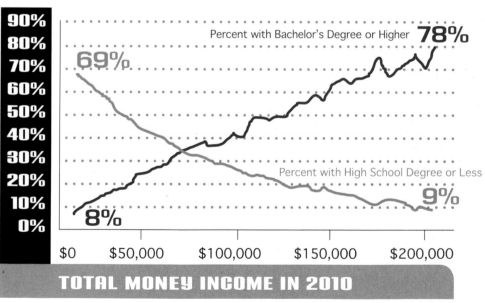

Percent with Bachelor's Degree or Higher **78%**

69%

Percent with High School Degree or Less

9%

8%

90% 80% 70% 60% 50% 40% 30% 20% 10% 0%

$0 $50,000 $100,000 $150,000 $200,000

TOTAL MONEY INCOME IN 2010

Source: Census and http://taxfoundation.org/article/who-are-americas-millionaires#_ftn5

Here's something to think about when you go off to college. The average starting salary for college grads in 2014 was $45,473.

HERE'S THE AVERAGE BY MAJOR:

>**BUSINESS: $53,901**

>**COMMUNICATIONS: $43,924**

>**COMPUTER SCIENCE: $61,741**

>**EDUCATION: $40,863**

>**ENGINEERING: $62,719**

>**HEALTH SCIENCES: $51,541**

>**HUMANITIES AND SOCIAL SCIENCES: $38,365**

>**MATH AND SCIENCES: $43,414**

Source: National Association of Colleges and Employers Salary Survey, April 2014
https://www.naceweb.org/uploadedFiles/Content/static-assets/downloads/executive-summary/2014-april-salary-survey-executive-summary.pdf

HOW MUCH $$$ DOES IT TAKE TO BE HAPPY?

Hank Williams Jr.

"Mo money, mo problems."
—BIGGIE SMALLS

"Well now, money can't buy you happiness, but neither can poor ole me."—HANK WILLIAMS JR.

Hank and Biggie were wrong. More money does not automatically equal more problems. And while you can't buy happiness with cold, hard cash, researchers have found that when people expand their income, they report more life satisfaction, no matter how much money they start with.

That's right—not if, but when. You can earn more than $1 million in your lifetime by following these tips.

1. Stay in school. Keep learning, whether it's college or a training program for a good job.

2. Know where your money goes. Track your spending and have a plan for your money. If you don't, you'll be surprised at how quickly it disappears.

3. Start saving. Because of the magic of compound interest, the earlier you start to save, the more your money will grow. Even putting aside a few dollars each paycheck is worthwhile.

4. Spend smart. If you spend nearly as much or more than you make, you'll have a hard time reaching seven-figure savings. Research before you buy and consider needs, wants, and long-term goals before shopping.

5. Take calculated risks. Dream big. Try new things. Don't be afraid to fail. But make sure the risks you're taking make sense and fit with your overall life plan.

MILLIONAIRE CALCULATOR

There's an easy online calculator for figuring how long it will take to earn $1 million, depending on the savings plan and amount saved per year. Check it out at themint.org.

Source: http://www.themint.org/kids/when-will-you-be-a-millionaire.html

While being a student is your primary job, paid work comes with benefits beyond a paycheck. A job can teach you responsibility, time management, teamwork, and how to keep commitments and manage money. These are lessons you'll use throughout life. They also come in handy for writing college application essays and deciding on a career.

Balancing work and school is a juggling act that requires support from your family and an organizational plan. Some ideas to keep you balanced include:

- *Keep a calendar of school and work commitments and consult the calendar before making plans.*

- *Stick to a weekly schedule, if possible, working the same number of hours and days.*

- *Start slowly. This will prevent overcommitting to work hours you can't handle.*

- *Ask your boss if you can use downtime at the job to do schoolwork. But don't count on downtime. When you're at work, the job comes first.*

- *If work is interfering with your success at school, you'll have to cut back on work.*

Jobs—what's HOT

The following jobs will be the 10 fastest-growing occupations between 2012 and 2022, according to the U.S. Bureau of Labor Statistics.

Source: http://www.bls.gov/ooh/fastest-growing.htm

OCCUPATION	GROWTH RATE	2012 MEDIAN PAY
Industrial-organizational psychologists	53 percent	$83,580
Personal care aides	49 percent	$19,910
Home health aides	48 percent	$20,820
Insulation workers, mechanical	47 percent	$39,170
Interpreters & translators	46 percent	$45,430
Diagnostic medical sonographers	46 percent	$65,860
Construction helpers*	43 percent	$28,220
Occupational therapy assistants	43 percent	$53,240
Genetic counselors	41 percent	$56,800
Physical therapist assistants	41 percent	$52,160

* Brickmasons, blockmasons, stonemasons, and tile and marble setters

GENERAL

FULL TIME 9-
CLERK POSITIC

GENERAL

OFFICE HELP
Seeking energetic & positive people. Excellent pay!
omotions available.

POOR WORK

FINDING A JOB

Having fun money is tops on teens' lists of reasons for getting a part-time job. Saving for college is important too.

But finding a part-time job can be challenging. The teen unemployment rate has stayed above 20 percent since the Great Recession of 2007–2009. You can look for a job through help-wanted ads in the newspaper, online at sites such as indeed.com or monster.com, or by searching for notices on bulletin boards or signs in storefronts.

If you don't find a job scooping ice cream or selling clothes at the mall, it's OK to ask around. Networking is an important skill and a common way for adults to find new opportunities. Ask your friends, people you know through school or extracurricular activities, your neighbors, and your family for ideas. The more people who know you're job-hunting and know the kinds of opportunities that interest you, the more likely you'll find the perfect job.

If you can't find a paid position, consider taking an unpaid internship in a field you are interested in or volunteering for a cause you care about. Either experience will look great on a résumé and may give you a better idea of what college major or career field would be the perfect fit for you. If money is a must, try to earn some by starting your own business babysitting, mowing lawns, or using a specialized skill such as developing websites or playing an instrument.

Don't forget to highlight your work or volunteer experiences in your college applications and essays. Holding down commitments outside of school while excelling in your studies shows a strong work ethic and the ability to succeed under pressure. They are qualities college admissions officers like to see.

WORKING FOR EXPERIENCE

Sometimes when you're young and exploring careers, you won't be paid for your work. Internships can offer excellent experience and help narrow down the type of career you will find fulfilling and enjoyable. Same with job shadowing, where you find someone whose job sounds interesting and ask to spend some time understanding what he or she does. That may mean heading to the office for the day, tagging along on sales visits, or spending the day in a classroom or doctor's office watching what the employee does. You might help with some tasks, but often job shadowing is what it sounds like—you are that person's "shadow" for the day. In many cases you won't get paid for doing this. Yet the experience, knowledge, and connections are worth a great deal.

For some positions, such as a store sales clerk or a restaurant server, you'll fill out an application form for the hiring manager. If the manager thinks you might be a good fit for the job, the application will be used as a starting point for an interview.

For other jobs you will need a résumé. It is a one-page document designed to help you sell your background, skills, education, and qualifications for a job. You need a rock-star résumé to stand out from the crowd. After all, you want the hiring manager's first impression to be "wow," not "meh."

- *Your name and contact information*
- *Summary statement about why you want the job*
- *Work and volunteer experience and internships*
- *Education, additional skills, and interests*
- *Honors and awards you've received*

Application for Employment

...modations for persons with disabilities...
...us know, and we will provide assistance.

Date of Application

First Name

City

...ears of age or over?

Date of Birth

While you'll have a standard résumé, you'll want to tweak it each time you apply for a new job so that it relates to that particular position. You'll also want to make sure your résumé is well written. No typos, poor grammar, or run-on sentences. Everything on a résumé must be accurate—no exaggerating or embellishing experience. Find a teacher, parent, or other adult to read your résumé and make suggestions before e-mailing or sending it to a potential employer. Collegeboard.com has good tips on writing a résumé. Job search site monster.com has sample résumés from many industries. If you are stuck, careerkids.com has a questionnaire that will spit out a basic résumé for you.

You may also need to submit a cover letter, which summarizes why you want the job and what makes you a good candidate. Employers might ask for references—people who can vouch for your character and experience. References are typically teachers, former co-workers, and adults who know you from volunteer or extracurricular settings.

Jane S. Doe
1234 Elm Street
Anytown, NY 12345
Phone: (123) 555-1234
E-mail: jsdoe@email.com

OBJECTIVE
To obtain a part-time position where I can use my computer and customer service skills.

EDUCATION
Anytown High School, Anytown, NY
Entering 11th grade, fall semester
GPA 3.5
Classes taken include Spanish I and II, Accounting I and II, Computer Science,
Web Design, and Introduction to Marketing.

EMPLOYMENT
June 2013–May 2014
Sales/Customer Service—KwikeeCopy, 555 1st Street, Anytown, NY
Processed jobs, maintained equipment, ordered supplies, answered phones, and
provided customer service.

OTHER WORK EXPERIENCE
2010–Present
Babysitting
Provide part-time child care for groups of one to four children.

VOLUNTEER EXPERIENCE
September 2013—Volunteered at Anytown Boys' and Girls' Club carnival.
March 2014—Organized charity car wash for Anytown Animal Shelter, which raised $500.

SPECIALIZED SKILLS
• Proficient with Microsoft Office software, including web design.
• Proficient with all types of social media.
• Fluent in Spanish.
• Work well and communicate effectively with a variety of people, including supervisors,
  co-workers, and customers.

HONORS AND AWARDS
• Elected sophomore class representative, Anytown High School.
• Named to honor roll each semester of freshman and sophomore years.
• Elected treasurer of Anytown High School Spanish Club.

EXTRACURRICULAR ACTIVITIES
Enjoy tennis, knitting, dog training, reading, and computer games.

REFERENCES
Available on request.

One of the hardest parts of landing a job is over—you have an interview. But what do you say at that interview? How should you act? Remember that you only get one chance to make a first impression—and you want to show the interviewer your best possible self.

Get smart: Since you've landed an interview, chances are you've done your research and know a lot about the company and job you hope to do. If not, this is your next step. Most companies have Internet and social media sites. You can also check the website of your local newspaper for articles about the company. Do not go to the interview unprepared or misinformed.

Be on time: Being punctual is as important as getting smart, if not more so.

Put on your listening ears: Pay careful attention to the questions you are asked. Ask for clarification if necessary.

Make eye contact: It's as important as ever, even in the age of texting and remote workplaces.

Play it safe: Interviews are generally not the place to discuss politics or religion, or to flaunt your expert knowledge of urban slang.

Follow-up: You may think that once you say your good-byes, all you have to do is wait. But if you want to increase your odds of landing the job, you have one more chance to make a good impression. Send a thank-you letter as soon as you can, preferably the same day. Express your thanks for being interviewed. Take the opportunity to briefly remind the interviewer of your skills, highlight a good point you made in the interview (or forgot to make), and add a final thank-you.

While e-mail is common these days, taking the extra step of also mailing a note on nice stationery or a note card will make a longer-lasting impression. Address the note to the person who interviewed you. And send a note even if you know right away that you didn't get the position. There's always next time.

WHAT (NOT) TO WEAR:
TEEN JOB INTERVIEW EDITION

Dress for success. That's a statement you've probably heard before. But what does it mean? Appropriate attire for the workplace will vary depending on the job. Some jobs have uniforms, making it easy to figure out what to wear. Without a uniform, knowing what to wear to work can be tricky. Almost every workplace has a dress code. When you go in for your interview, you will be able to see how employees are dressed.

But wait—how do you know what to wear to a job interview? Or more important, what NOT to wear?

Again, it will vary. If you're interviewing at an investment firm, chances are women wear skirts, dresses, or suits, and men might wear suits and ties. If you are interviewing at an advertising agency, outfits probably vary based on personal style, and many styles are acceptable. When in doubt, dress up, not down. Here are some other suggestions, especially if you're applying for an office job:

Just ask: Talk to the person setting up the interview about the workplace atmosphere and how people typically dress.

Don't wear jeans: In most cases wearing jeans to an interview is a no-no, even if jeans are acceptable in the workplace. Keep the sneakers at home too, even your best pair.

Don't wear jeans, unless … : You are applying to work retail at a store that sells exclusively jeans. It's OK to tweak your style based on the merchandise and atmosphere of the store you're hoping will hire you. But don't go overboard.

Be conservative: No bra straps showing, no see-through clothing, nothing too tight, nothing too short.

Have fun: Being conservative doesn't mean boring. You can wear color, jewelry (but not too much bling), or patterns that let your personal style shine through.

No hats: Sorry, kids.

Accessorize: Always bring your résumé and any samples of your work.

Not seen, not heard: Keep the smartphones and tablets out of sight.

CHAPTER TWO

BEING YOUR
OWN BOSS

"You're not the boss of me!"

Almost every kid has uttered that sentence at one point. The idea of being free to do what you want and make your own decisions has appeal no matter how old you are. It's one reason why 11.5 million Americans have chosen to be entrepreneurs instead of working for someone else.

But running a small business is hard work. It takes a good idea, a business plan, start-up money, and more. So where to begin?

WOULDN'T IT BE COOL IF ...

The first step is coming up with an idea. Ideas come from all over the place—a frustration you've experienced, an opportunity you've uncovered, or a dream that awakens you in the middle of the night with an "aha" moment. But before you go too far with your idea, ask yourself the following questions:

- *How do I like to spend my time?*

- *How much time do I have?*

- *What are my strongest skills?*

- *What do others say I am good at?*

- *Can any of this translate into a moneymaking opportunity?*

Once you've come up with an idea, survey the landscape. Identify the need you're fulfilling. Check to see if there are other local businesses already doing what you're planning to do. If there is competition, how will you drum up business? How will your business be different or better?

Still convinced you have a good idea? Running your business will take a lot of time, dedication, and sacrifice. Be honest with yourself and ask the following questions:

- *Would you rather work on your business than play sports, act in the school play, or watch TV?*

- *Would you rather spend your money on your business instead of on clothes or other wants and desires?*

- *Do you realistically have the time it will take without jeopardizing your studies? School, after all, is your primary job. Will family and friends help you out?*

If you are still jazzed about the idea of running a business, work your way through the handy pre-business checklist on the next page. It's from the U.S. Small Business Administration (SBA).

- *What services or products will I sell? Where will I be located?*

- *What skills and experience do I bring to the business?*

- *What will I name my business?*

- *What equipment or supplies will I need?*

- *What insurance coverage will be needed?*

- *How much money, if any, will it cost to start my business? Will I need financing?*

- *What are my resources?*

- *How will I compensate myself?*

Once you've walked yourself through the questions and checklist on the previous pages, it's time to get it all down in a formal document called a business plan. The purpose of a business plan is to define your business, as well as your strategy for establishing the business, keeping it going, and reaching the goals you outlined. It's the game plan for your business vision.

The business plan will draw from all of the research you've already completed. The SBA has another handy checklist that shows what should be included in the business plan. Find it at the SBA website, http://archive.sba.gov/teens/.

Here's a peek at a few of the items on the list:

- **Give a detailed description of the business and its goals.**

- **Discuss the advantages you and your business have over your competitors.**

- **Identify the customer demand for your product or service.**

- **Identify your market, its size, and its locations.**

- **Explain how your product or service will be advertised and marketed.**

- **Explain the pricing strategy.**

- **Decide the amount and source of initial capital (money) you'll need.**

- Develop a monthly operating budget for the first year.

- Determine your break-even point where your income will at least cover your expenses. Anything above that is profit.

- Explain how the business will be managed on a day-to-day basis.

- Account for the equipment necessary to produce your products or services.

IDEA, PLAN, FINANCE

Once you've come up with a business idea and written your plan, your next step is to put that plan into action. Figuring out the financing—how you're going to pay for the business—is usually a key piece of the plan. If your business is going to require outside capital, there are several ways to raise it:

- *Use personal savings and earnings. Many entrepreneurs don't pay themselves a salary for many months, if not years. They put their earnings back into the business instead.*

- *Ask for start-up funds from family or friends.*

- *Ask your peers for help using a crowdfunding site such as Kickstarter.com or a peer-to-peer lending site such as lendingclub.com.*

- *Apply for a bank loan.*

Mik Bushinski's cool life revolves around ice time and ice cream.

Bushinski needed a summer job that would allow him to attend hockey practice and work out twice a day. When he couldn't find one, he started a business selling ice cream treats in his Woodbury, Minnesota, subdivision. That was five years ago. Now he's 20 and has expanded his business from a single ice cream minivan to multiple vehicles and an ice cream vending machine business. Here's his story:

Mik Bushinski

He looked for an unmet need: "We had lived in Woodbury for close to 20 years and hadn't seen ice cream trucks very often and knew the community was growing and had a lot of families with children, so it seemed like a good fit."

He found start-up capital: "I needed about $5,000 to get the business started. My uncle gave me a no-interest loan."

He had a goal: "My ultimate motivation was to be able to keep playing hockey at Shattuck-St. Mary's for my high school career, and I needed to be able to help with the cost of that."

He got help from his family: "In the second year I added a second truck, which my parents and brother helped run. Then last year my little sister got a truck and is now running that one. We got a professional logo last year and had it put on all of the trucks, and we professionalized our website. We ventured into the ice cream vending business (my little sister handles most of that), and we hire a few people to help out in the summer."

MIK'S ADVICE FOR BUDDING ENTREPRENEURS:

1. Find a product that you believe in and would buy yourself.
2. Be ready to put a lot of time into your own business.
3. Make sure you have a financial plan.

Isaiah Rusk of Houston, Texas, started his own retail business at age 15, after his friends kept asking for style advice.

The business plan:

"I can go to the thrift store, pick up things that are cool, and post them on a website, and if they like it, they could buy it."

His start-up capital:

"I saved up. It took me several months to get what I needed."

Isaiah Rusk

His marketing plan:

"I got the word out through Twitter and Instagram and Tumblr. Most of my customers aren't even from my area."

How he juggles a business and school:

He shops on Friday after school or Saturday, restocks the store on Sunday, and sends out orders "after I do my homework."

Where he went for business advice:

The Junior Achievement organization and his mom, who is also an entrepreneur.

ISAIAH'S ADVICE TO ENTREPRENEURS:

1. When you get some money, you can't just blow it all. Most of the time you've got to put it to the side. Certain things will come up and you have to pay.
2. Be patient.
3. Don't involve your friends.

Plan for the future: He said he hopes to expand his website "to maybe like a small store, not necessarily a chain store, but just a small store. But what I mainly focus on is my acting. You always have to have some sort of backup plan when you're trying to be an actor."

What does it take to be an ENTREPRENEUR?

Entrepreneurs need ... ZOG. Entrepreneurs need zest, optimism, and grit, according to Camp BizSmart blogger Peggy Gibbs.

"Zest is defined as living life with a sense of excitement, anticipation, and energy. ... Zest is essentially the courage, and self motivation to complete challenging situations and tasks. Optimism is a positive, 'Can Do Attitude,' about life, school and work. ... Train yourself to see solutions, not just problems. Grit is sticking with things over the very long term until you master them."

CHAPTER THREE

WAGES
AND TAXES

Earning money is not just about an hourly wage, where you receive a certain amount of money for each hour on the job. There are various types of compensation. For example, you could earn a salary, which is a fixed amount of money you earn no matter how many hours you work per week. A salary is paid at regular periods, usually every other week or twice each month.

You may also work on commission, which means you are paid for completing certain tasks or reaching a goal. Commission is often tied to a sales goal.

Service workers often receive tips, which is money earned on top of a base wage because of a job well done or because of social convention. The consumer—the person being served—pays the tip. In some occupations, such as restaurant server and taxi driver, tips tend to be given regardless of the quality of the work. But remember that tips aren't mandatory and can fluctuate based on whether the consumer thinks you did a lousy job or a lovely one.

Is there a certain amount an employer must pay you? It depends. The United States has a minimum wage for most workers. That amount is currently $7.25 an hour. Congress must pass legislation to change it, although states can require businesses to pay a higher minimum wage. For example, workers making minimum wage in the state of Washington earn $9.32 per hour.

better
power
strong
effective
families
women
supporters
changed

pay
minimum
hard
jurisdictions
labor
ge

Not all workers are paid minimum wage. Employers can pay workers who are younger than 20 a minimum wage of $4.25 per hour during their first 90 days on the job. Teens who babysit or are full-time students don't have to be paid minimum wage. If you receive tips on the job, you might not be paid minimum wage, depending on the amount of tips received. The U.S. Department of Labor website at http://www.dol.gov has all of the details.

EARNING MONEY IN YOUR SLEEP

Who wants to earn some money without lifting a finger? Who wouldn't raise their hand? The good news is that there are ways to watch your money grow over time without having to do much.

How? One of the best ways to earn money is by saving money in an account that earns interest.

Interest is money paid to someone who has agreed to let another party put their money to use for whatever purpose. When you open a savings account at a bank or credit union, you will be paid a small amount of interest for giving them your money and allowing them to use it for lending or other purposes. The interest paid is calculated as a percentage based on how much money you've deposited.

Where can you earn interest? In savings accounts, for sure. But there are also interest-earning options in college savings plans called 529 plans and tax-free individual retirement accounts (IRAs), which are designed to save for retirement.

GETTING BY WITH A LITTLE HELP FROM FRIENDS (AND STRANGERS)

Banks aren't the only places you can earn interest. You can act as the bank yourself, lending money to your family members, friends, or even complete strangers through peer-to-peer lending. Peer-to-peer lending is just what it sounds like. It's been happening for centuries, but the Internet makes it possible to bring together strangers living in various parts of the world to help each other reach their financial goals. This marketplace has grown a lot in recent years, as banks made it tougher for consumers to borrow money and also cut interest rates paid on savings accounts. The conditions forced consumers looking for loans and consumers looking to earn interest to seek alternatives outside of banks. Peer-to-peer lending was born.

Websites such as prosper.com and lendingclub.com act as marketplaces for people looking for money and people looking to earn interest by lending money. Lenders who have money to offer browse the website. They read descriptions of borrowers—people who need a loan. Lenders learn who the borrowers are, where they live, why they're asking for cash, and how likely it is that they will be able to pay back the loan. Lenders will receive a certain amount of interest in return for lending their money to borrowers.

Money isn't the only thing that you can lend in return for cash[...]
[...]k about how many items you can rent in this society—apart[...]
[...], lawn equipment, bikes, prom dresses, movies, and TV show[...]
[...] own property people would pay to use, that's another way to [...]
[...]ey without doing a job or waiting for interest to build.

That first paycheck is a thrill. But wait—why does it look so small? Taxes. Social Security. Medicare. The cost of benefits. It doesn't take long to realize that your hourly wage and your take-home pay are not the same thing. The actual amount in your paycheck that you get to spend? That's your net pay. It's what you have left after your employer withholds all of the mandatory stuff such as federal and state income taxes, and the voluntary deductions such as retirement savings and some types of insurance premiums. Your pay before all of the deductions is called your gross pay—as in, bigger than it was before all of those deductions kicked in, or isn't it gross that my paycheck is so much smaller?

In all seriousness, taxes benefit society by raising money to fix roads, keep parks beautiful, and protect citizens during wars and at home. Taxes are mandatory, and you must pay taxes on the income that you earn. If you're an employee of a company, the company will take a percentage of your salary each month to pay for state and federal taxes and programs such as Social Security and Medicare. Think of Social Security as a government-sponsored plan that gives retirees and select others a small monthly paycheck. Medicare is the government-sponsored health care plan for those 65 years old or older. If you see the term FICA (Federal Insurance Contributions Act) on your paycheck, it's referring to these programs.

Your paycheck may also have deductions that aren't required by the government. The voluntary deductions include health, disability, and life insurance; benefits that reduce the cost of child care or work-related parking expenses; and company retirement plans.

WHAT GETS TAKEN OUT OF YOUR PAYCHECK?

FEDERAL INCOME TAX

- The amount withheld based on taxable income, pay frequency, marital status, and the number of dependents claimed

SOCIAL SECURITY

- Flat percentage deducted based on taxable income

- May appear on your paycheck as FICA

MEDICARE TAX

- Flat percentage deducted based on taxable income

- May appear on your paycheck as FICA

OTHER DEDUCTIONS

- Insurance policies that vary based on employer or state policy

STATE INCOME TAX

- Based on your W-4 and/or state income tax form *

- Based on taxable income, marital status, and dependents

There are five common payroll deductions made from an employee's earnings:

X COMPANY
Anytown, CA

Earnings Statement

Social Security Number: 999-99-9999
Taxable Marital Status: Single

Jane S. Doe
1234 Elm Street
Anytown, CA 12345

EARNINGS	Rate	Hours	This Period
Regular	$10.00	40.00	$400.00
Overtime	$15.00	1.00	$15.00
Gross Pay			$415.00

DEDUCTIONS	Statutory	
	Federal Income Tax	$42.00
	Social Security	$17.43
	Medicare Tax	$6.02
	Other Deductions	$15.00
	State Income Tax	$17.00
Net Pay		$317.55

* Not all states have state income tax.

If you've used allowance or birthday money to buy toys, clothes, or video games, or even eaten at a restaurant, you've likely paid sales tax. Sales tax is a set rate, no matter who you are or how much money you make. Depending on the state where you live, some items, such as groceries or clothes, might not be subject to sales tax. But most things you buy in a store are taxed.

Income tax is different. The amount of money withheld from your paycheck for taxes depends on how much you earn. It generally increases as you earn more. When you start your job, your employer will have you fill out a W-4 form, which tells your employer how much money to withhold from your paycheck and send to the IRS. Your parents or guardians or your employer can help you fill out that short form.

Teens don't always earn enough to have to file an annual income tax return. But it's worth considering, because a refund may be waiting from the government.

22222	Void ☐	a Employee's social security number	For Official Use Only ▶ OMB No. 1545-0008		
b Employer identification number (EIN)				1 Wages, tips, other compensation	2 Federal income tax withheld
c Employer's name, address, and ZIP code				3 Social security wages	4 Social security tax withheld
				5 Medicare wages and tips	6 Medicare tax withheld
				7 Social security tips	8 Allocated tips
d Control number				9	10 Dependent care benefits
e Employee's first name and initial	Last name		Suff.	11 Nonqualified plans	12a See instructions for box 12
				13 Statutory employee ☐ Retirement plan ☐ Third-party sick pay ☐	12b
				14 Other	12c
					12d
f Employee's address and ZIP code					
15 State Employer's state ID number	16 State wages, tips, etc.	17 State income tax	18 Local wages, tips, etc.	19 Local income tax	20 Locality name

Form **W-2** Wage and Tax Statement   **2014**   Department of the Treasury—Internal Revenue Service

Copy A For Social Security Administration — Send this entire page with Form W-3 to the Social Security Administration; photocopies are **not** acceptable.

For Privacy Act and Paperwork Reduction Act Notice, see the separate instructions.

Cat. No. 10134D

Do Not Cut, Fold, or Staple Forms on This Page

Source: http://www.irs.gov/pub/irs-pdf/fw2.pdf

The income tax form is called a 1040. Young people can typically use the simpler 1040EZ form to file. To help you prepare that form, your employer will send you a W-2 Wage and Tax Statement at the beginning of each year. The W-2 includes the wages and tips you earned during the previous year, as well as the taxes withheld.

Want to earn more money? Who doesn't? As you get older and expenses rise, you'll need to steadily increase your salary to maintain your investment goals and standard of living. Sometimes you'll be offered a raise or promotion for working hard and gaining more experience. Other times you'll have to make a case for why you should earn more money.

Negotiating a salary or raise can be nerve-wracking, especially the first time. If you're still receiving an allowance from your parents or guardians, you can test your negotiating skills by asking for an increase in the amount you receive.

When you're ready to ask for more money at work or at home, follow these tips:

- *Treat your employer with respect. That goes for Mom and Dad too.*

- *Come to the table with a number in mind. Do your research. If negotiating an allowance, ask your friends how much allowance they are paid and for what sorts of tasks. If you're employed, find out what other workers in similar jobs are making. Check websites such as salary.com, indeed.com, or glassdoor.com for general information. But don't ask your co-workers what they are making. Most employers consider this information confidential. Also, don't forget that cost of living is different depending on where you live. That means employers may pay more or less based on location. Check out a cost-of-living calculator, available on most salary websites.*

- *Your magic number? Don't share it right away, especially if you're in the midst of negotiating an initial salary. And don't tell potential employers exactly how much you've made in past jobs. You might feel as if you have to if you're asked, but revealing that number could lower your salary offer at the new job. Of course, if you're negotiating at an existing job or for your allowance, this rule doesn't apply.*

- *Consider how your responsibilities have changed or your quality of work has improved. Would you be willing to take on more work for the raise you're proposing?*

- *If you're negotiating your allowance and don't earn money based on specific chores, make the case for more cash by analyzing your expenses and explaining what has changed in your financial life that requires more allowance.*

- *Dissatisfied with the results of your negotiation? Tell your employer or parent or guardian that the number is lower than your expectations, and ask how he or she settled on that figure. Or request a plan to improve your performance or add skills so you have a greater chance of receiving a raise the next time you ask.*

IT PAYS TO NEGOTIATE

People who don't negotiate their first salary could lose more than $500,000 in earnings from the time they start their career until they reach age 60, according to statistics compiled by Linda Babcock, author of *Women Don't Ask*.

The term "gig economy" refers to the growing number of Americans who are working on a per-project or freelance basis. Often in the gig economy, a person has mini-jobs. The worker might work a few hours on one project and perform an entirely different task for another project.

Some people work in the gig economy by choice. Working on multiple projects can keep work interesting and help develop a variety of useful skills. The gig economy is flexible, giving workers more freedom to work when and where they want. But there are also many workers in the gig economy who would like a full-time permanent job but can't find one.

More people joined the gig economy during the Great Recession of 2007–2009, when employers reduced costs by laying off workers or hiring temporary help. New businesses such as TaskRabbit popped up. TaskRabbit.com matches people who need help with odd jobs with people who are looking to earn a little cash.

In better economic times, fewer workers tend to work on a per-project basis as companies start hiring permanent employees again. However, advances in technology that make it easier for workers to work remotely, and a growing number of people who want a better work-life balance, point to the gig economy's permanent place in the work world.

Most of us have many ideas about what we want to be as we grow older and our interests change. Picking a career that we like and that will allow us to earn a good income is the key to success. Do well in high school and earn a college degree in a major with good job prospects, and you're likely to find more career opportunities.

If you are itching to be your own boss, there are many resources out there to help you, from Junior Achievement to the volunteer mentors of the Small Business Administration's SCORE Association. Just think, all major corporations once started with the kernel of an idea.

An idea, an entrepreneurial spirit, perseverance, and hard work can take you far. And always remember that millionaires who spend more than they make are worse off than average people who live within their means. Saving money and making savvy decisions about the money you spend are just as important as earning it.

MAKE IT A HABIT

From the time we're old enough to understand that money buys toys, movies, and the latest must-have pair of jeans, we are ready to shop. There are so many desirable things to have. When we walk by stores, check out online photos of what our friends bought at the mall, or see a celebrity carrying a certain smartphone or wearing designer sunglasses, our brains shout, "I want, I want, I want!"

It would be so easy to spend all of our money on new things and good times. One of the most important things to learn as you get older, gain responsibilities, and have access to more money is the importance of saving. There are many places, ways, and reasons to save. It can be overwhelming, but don't worry. This book will help you understand the basics of accumulating cash. And the sooner you make saving a habit, the richer you'll be.

CHAPTER FOUR

SAVVY SAVING

Pay yourself first. Maybe you've heard this simple phrase before. But what does it mean? When you get your paycheck, before you cover your cell phone bill or make plans to go out with friends, set aside some money in savings. That's what it means.

Paying yourself first is a way to put your financial security before your wants. Try to keep the cost of your needs low enough that you can pay yourself first, cover your expenses, and still have fun.

But there's more to saving than just deciding to put money away. You must decide where to save, what you are saving for, and when you will need to access the money.

WHY SAVE?

Let's face it. Saving probably is not the first thing you'd like to do with your money, but it's necessary. We save money to afford purchases we plan to make. Some of those purchases will be for things we want and some for things we need. But we also save money to plan for the unexpected.

When you save money, you give up the opportunity to do something else with it, such as spend it or give it away. This is known as opportunity cost.

Because saving isn't the most fun thing in the world, many of us need to come up with ways to persuade us to save. For some, the security of having money "just in case" is incentive enough. For others, it's the challenge of meeting a goal. Then there are those who are driven to save because they like to see their fortune grow or not have to ask their parents for money to buy a new phone. As in most financial decisions, people have very different ideas about how to manage their savings. They come up with reasons and amounts to save based on their wants and needs.

Putting your goals in order

If only there was unlimited money, like a pot of gold at the end of the rainbow. But since there isn't, you need to decide what to save for and how much you can afford to set aside for that goal. Chances are you have more than one savings goal. You might want to save for a new video game, a spring break trip, car insurance, and college tuition. And while you might not be thrilled with the idea, it's wise to start saving for retirement now.

How do you figure out how to save for everything? First you determine how much money you have to save after paying for today's needs and wants. Then it's a matter of dividing up the money that's left. Financial experts suggest trying to save at least 10 percent of your income for retirement. Some say you need to save 20 percent to be safe. If that's too much, start small. Even $20 a month will add up over time.

WHERE TO SAVE?

Banks accept deposits of money from customers. They also lend money to customers. Banks are for-profit institutions and charge interest to people taking out loans. They also may pay interest to people depositing money, depending on what type of account they have. Interest is your payment for allowing the bank to lend your money to other customers.

The interest is calculated as a percentage based on how much money you've deposited.

General savings accounts are designed to save for all sorts of reasons. Other accounts are designed to save for particular goals, such as college and retirement. These specialized accounts tend to have tax benefits. But they also tend to have restrictions on how you can use them, so you need to be sure before you open one that you won't need the money for something else.

Savings account: A savings account is versatile, easy to access, and designed to save money for any purpose. But because the interest rate earned is low, it's best for emergency savings and short-term savings goals.

IRA: An individual retirement account has tax advantages that lower your tax bill today. It can be used in some circumstances for a home down payment or college tuition, but it's mainly considered a retirement account.

401(k), 403(b), 457 plans: Various workplace retirement plans are set up for you by your employer. You designate a percentage of your paycheck to go into that account. Some employers will contribute a matching amount to the account, usually up to a certain percentage.

529 plans: Savers use 529 plans to save for college. They must be used for college expenses.

ROTH IRA: A Roth IRA is funded with money left after you pay taxes. It can only be funded with money you earn from working. It's designed to lower your tax bill in the future. This fund is much more versatile than the IRA, because you can withdraw the money you contribute to the fund for any purpose at any time. This makes it good for saving for retirement, college, or a house. And if you don't tap it for other purposes, you will have money for retirement. It's like the little black dress of savings.

Brokerage accounts: Brokerage accounts let you invest in any number of things—from individual stocks to mutual funds. These accounts can be used for any purpose.

Emergency savings: Rainy day fund. Cash cushion. These are terms used to describe money you save just in case something unexpected or unfortunate happens. An emergency savings account should be opened at a bank or credit union and should not be used as fun money, even if you're tempted.

What are some examples of acceptable expenses for this type of account? Paying for an unexpectedly high heating bill in your first apartment. Replacing a lost textbook. Repairing a bike tire. But while it's OK to use this type of account to fix items you own, repairs aren't exactly emergencies. You should anticipate and budget for the cost of repairs and routine maintenance of bikes, appliances, cars, and homes. So how much emergency savings should you have? If you're just getting started, pick an achievable goal—$1,000, $500, or even $50—and an amount to save from each paycheck or allowance. It's OK to start small.

WHEN TO SAVE

Some places to save are better than others, depending on when you'll need the money. This is called your time horizon. Before picking your account, you must ask yourself whether you need your money very soon (in the next year), in the short term (less than three years), medium term (three to five years), or long term (five or more years). This will help you decide whether to save in a bank account or to take on more risk by investing your money in stocks.

short term

medium term

long term

Bet you didn't think physics had any application to saving, did you? But the law of inertia—that objects at rest tend to stay at rest and objects in motion tend to stay in motion—can be the difference between retiring one day and working until you drop. Inertia is derived from the Latin word *iners*, which means idle or lazy. What behavioral economists have found is that inertia can be a positive force in savings, but only if you can manage to get started.

Let's say you just landed your first job. Your employer will ask you where you want to deposit your paycheck. It's typical to divide your paycheck into more than one account, such as a checking account and a savings account. You could decide to have 10 percent of your salary automatically deposited into a savings account each month. Or you could decide to put money in a savings account on your own if you have money left over after paying expenses. Which choice increases your odds of successfully saving? You guessed it—the first choice. By setting up your paycheck so you automatically save each payday, you are using inertia to your benefit. If you say you'll take care of it later, you may never get around to setting up that savings account.

It can be challenging, but it's important to get into the habit of saving. The earlier you do, the better. As you get older, you'll likely encounter unexpected expenses, and you will need a cash cushion to ensure a soft landing.

INFLATION

Your grandparents probably tell stories about how items cost a lot less when they were young, such as candy bars that sold for a nickel. You'd have a hard time finding a candy bar for that price today. Prices for goods and services increase over time. That's called inflation, and it can take a big bite out of your long-term savings. What cost $100 in 1993 costs about $162 today. A $100 bill in 1913 has the same buying power as $2,359 today. With luck, your salary will increase to keep up with inflation, but this isn't always the case. Inflation is just one reason why it's necessary to save.

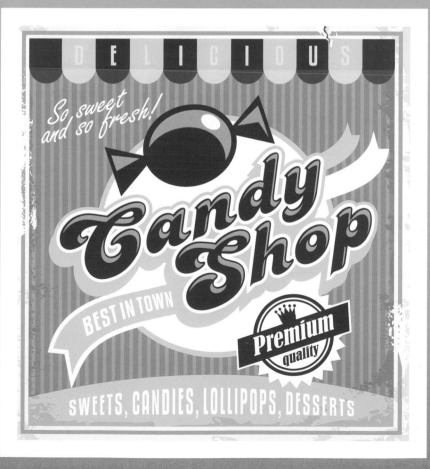

SAVINGS IN DISGUISE

You can positively punch up your bottom line in more ways than just sticking money in the bank. For example, when you pay off debt, you are essentially saving money. If you pay off a loan that charges 5 percent interest, you've just saved yourself the 5 percent you would have had to pay in the future on that loan.

Another way to save money is by spending less. Instead of buying an item the moment you see it, research prices and look for coupons. The less you pay, the more money you've saved. Finally, there's the choice to not buy something in the first place. Many wants fade if you decide to sit on a purchase for a while.

PATIENCE + PERSEVERANCE = FULL POCKETBOOK!

That is financial planner Therese R. Nicklas' equation for financial success.

What does this mean? Nicklas says in order to succeed at achieving financial goals, you need two key ingredients—patience and perseverance. "Patience means before making a purchase, give yourself the 24-hour test. Wait 24 hours before buying something. If the craving passes, you really didn't need the item. Persevere and keep your eye on the prize!"

Break your goal down to manageable pieces, says Nicklas, a Boston-area certified financial planner. She gives this example: Say you have a goal of joining your high school class on a European trip. The cost is $1,800. It is September 1, and you just learned of this opportunity. The trip will take place in April, and you need to have your final payment in by March 31. EVERYONE is going.

You approach your parents with your best sales pitch, and they say flat out, "No, we can't afford it. College is right around the corner!" So what do you do? Give up, keep begging—hoping to wear them down—or figure out how to raise the money yourself? Let's hope you choose the latter, and here is what you will need to do. It is as easy as 1, 2, 3!

THREE-PART PLAN

Our imaginary high school student can follow Nicklas' three-part plan to raise money for the trip.

1. Create a timeline. You have seven months to raise $1,800, which equals about $257 per month. Looking at it another way, you have about 30 weeks to raise $1,800, which equals $60 per week.

In order to net $60 per week, you would need to work approximately 10 hours a week and earn approximately $8 per hour. (Don't forget tax withholding.) If you have other expenses besides your trip, you will need to earn more to cover them.

2. Get a job and create a savings plan. A

part-time job after school and on weekends should cover your needs. What special skills do you have that could earn you money? How about babysitting? Lawn mowing, computer repair (or computer lessons), or tutoring? A job in retail? Put on your thinking cap and let your imagination soar!

You know you need to save a minimum of $60 per week to achieve your goal. Set up a separate bank account for the trip. Either set up an automatic deposit to this account, or discipline yourself to go to the bank each week and make your deposit.

Your patience and perseverance will pay off! In no time you will see your bank account grow. Before you know it, you will be enjoying your European trip with the satisfaction that you did it yourself!

3. Create a lifestyle plan. Now that you achieved

this milestone, keep going. Don't stop!

Continue to save for other future goals, such as buying a car or contributing to your college education. Having a separate bank account for special goals makes it easier to discipline yourself to succeed.

You just taught yourself two valuable skills—paying yourself first and living within your means. Congratulations! You are on your way to enjoying a lifestyle of financial freedom!

"*A penny saved is a penny earned.*"

"*A small leak will sink a great ship.*"

"*For age and want, save while you may, no morning sun lasts a whole day.*"

Benjamin Franklin is best known as one of America's Founding Fathers, signer of the Declaration of Independence, publisher of *Poor Richard's Almanac*, and inventor of bifocals. But did you know he could be considered America's first financial guru?

As a newspaperman and printer, Franklin shared many common sense words of wisdom about saving, earning, and spending money. Many of the sayings are laid out in his 1758 essay *The Way to Wealth*. Do his quotes sound familiar?

The abandoned Wyndcliffe mansion on the Hudson River may have inspired the saying "Keeping up with the Joneses." Built in 1853, its first owner was Elizabeth Schermerhorn Jones.

KEEPING UP WITH THE JONESES

When people say they are "keeping up with the Joneses," they are comparing their lifestyle and possessions to those of their neighbors. Some say the idea of the Joneses came from a comic strip of the same name published in the early 1900s. Others say the phrase may have come from a wealthy New York family of that name in the mid-1800s.

Either way, trying to keep up with the stuff and spending habits of your friends and neighbors can get you into a lot of financial trouble. Besides, there's no way of knowing if your classmates or neighbors bought a new car with cash or with a high-interest loan they can barely afford.

CHAPTER FIVE

TAKING IT TO THE BANK

A piggy bank is a fine place to start saving. But at some point your savings will outgrow a ceramic pig. Instead of getting an even bigger piggy bank, most people trade up to the real thing—a bank.

Putting your money in the bank is safer than keeping it at home. It's also harder to spend your money if it's not right within reach. Banks give you lots of choices for how to save and access your money.

Your parents may have opened a savings account for you when you were young and deposited gift money into that account. The account was probably at their bank, because having your account there was convenient for them.

CHOOSING A BANK

When you're ready to start managing your own money, think about what's important to you in a financial institution. All banks have FDIC insurance, which means that up to $250,000 of your deposits are guaranteed, even in the rare event that the bank would fail. All banks provide checks, access to ATMs, and debit cards. Nearly all banks have online tools to help you keep track of your money and where it goes.

The options of checking your account balance with a text message and using an app to deposit birthday checks with your smartphone may make a bank located near you seem less important.

While some people like to have a bank location, called a branch, near their home, workplace, or school, fewer people visit bank branches today than in the past. If you like to handle your banking online or by smartphone, a nearby location may be less important than a bank with the latest online and mobile banking tools.

Some banks offer new customers incentives for opening an account and keeping it open for a certain period of time. Banks used to give items such as toasters as account-opening gifts. Today the gifts are more likely to be cash or gift cards. If you're having a tough time deciding between financial institutions, consider one that gives you a bonus for opening the account. Some banks will give you $100 for opening a new account and depositing money. That will give you a head start toward your savings goals.

CREDIT UNIONS

Opening an account at a bank isn't your only option. Like a bank, a credit union keeps your money safe, provides access to your money when needed, and offers loans. But credit unions are not-for-profit, and the users of a credit union are its members who typically have a vote in some credit union decisions.

Credit unions tend to be smaller, are usually locally run, and may limit who becomes a member. For example, you might have to live in a particular community or work at a certain company. Whether you pick a bank or a credit union is up to you. Either way, your money will be safe.

THE MAGIC OF COMPOUND INTEREST

Various types of interest calculations determine how much money you will earn on the money in your account. The most basic calculation is simple interest, which is calculated only on the money you initially deposited in the account.

To earn more on your money, open an account that pays interest using compound interest. With compound interest, you earn interest on the cash in your account and on any interest you've previously earned. The more often your bank calculates your compound interest, the faster your money will multiply. An account compounding interest four times a year is better than an account that compounds once each year.

For doing nothing but keeping your money in the bank, you earn money. Without lifting a finger. And every time you are paid interest, the amount of interest paid gets bigger. This is why it's so important to start saving for retirement as soon as you can. Your money will start small but grow sizably over time.

Compound interest plays a big role in being able to retire. Your money has more chances to compound if you start saving for retirement decades before you plan to stop working. It may seem crazy to put money away for retirement when you're still saving for your first car or paying for college. But you'd be crazy *not* to do it.

The tale of
TWO SAVERS

Tammy and Jerry are friends who are 65 years old and share a birthday. When Tammy was 25, she started an IRA and saved $100 a month for 40 years. The IRA produced average returns of 7 percent per year.

Jerry waited until he was 45 years old and doubled the contributions, putting aside $200 per month for 20 years. Both friends stopped saving on their 65th birthdays. Without calculating interest, the two friends saved an identical amount: $48,000. But when factoring in compound interest, who comes out ahead?

Tammy does. By a lot. Just by starting 20 years earlier and letting compound interest work its magic over a longer time period, Tammy ends up with $258,020. Jerry has just a little more than $103,000. The lesson: starting early with any dollar amount is smarter than waiting until you have enough money to save a larger amount.

CHAPTER SIX

INVESTING
BASICS

Investing can be a daunting topic for beginners, but it's really quite simple. The basic concept of investing is taking the money you have now and making it grow.

You can start with as little as $20 and can invest for many reasons—for the challenge, for the sense of owning something, or for the more practical purpose of making sure you have enough money in the future.

Generally, investments will earn you more than money sitting in a savings account will. Investments are designed for a time horizon that lasts years, not months. Some investments are riskier than others. Some investments are liquid, meaning it's easy to get your money out of the investment relatively quickly. Others are illiquid, meaning your money will be tough to access.

The return on an investment—what you get for investing the time or money in the first place—is not always measured in an exact dollar amount. For example, your education is an investment. Research shows that a four-year college degree is worth an average of more than $1 million in earning potential.

TYPES OF INVESTMENTS

STOCKS

Stocks allow people to buy small pieces, called shares, of a company. Companies sell stock to raise money for various purposes. The shares are bought and sold on a marketplace called an exchange. Most of the buying and selling a century ago took place on the stock market floor, but today most transactions occur electronically.

The value of stock shares can go up and down. It's possible to lose all of your money invested in a stock. But on average the stock market has increased in value.

When you own stock in a company, you are called a shareholder. You have a vested interest in how well the company does. When a company does well, its stock tends to go up, which means your shares are worth more if you were to sell them that day. If a company doesn't perform as well as expected, the value of the shares can go down, and your investment would be worth less. Since money invested in the stock market should have a longer time horizon, you should not worry if the market fluctuates. It only matters how much the stock is worth on the day you plan to sell it.

BONDS

A bond is essentially an IOU given to you by the company that sells the bond. When you buy a bond, the company agrees to pay back the money you lent plus interest on a certain date in the future. Some bonds are riskier than others and depend on the overall health of a company's finances. Bonds are considered safer than stocks, but it is possible to lose money on bonds.

MUTUAL FUNDS

A mutual fund is a collection of various types of investments. Think of it as a grocery bag that holds each of your financial food groups—a mix of stocks, bonds, and cash. Professional investors manage some mutual funds, charging fees to choose what goes in the grocery bag. They hope to fill it with investments that will grow the most over time. Other mutual funds track an index of stocks or bonds, buying a little bit of all the stocks or bonds on the index. Because these mutual funds, called index funds, don't have professionals picking the stocks or bonds to buy, index funds have lower fees.

SAVINGS BONDS

Chances are you've received a savings bond as a gift at some point in your life. The U.S. government sells the bonds to raise money. Savings bonds carry little risk, but their interest rate tends to be low.

PROPERTY

Investing opportunities exist outside of financial accounts. It isn't necessary to have millions of dollars in order to invest in a company or product. You could buy property. There are other types of property to buy besides a home or piece of land. You could invest in a snowblower and start a business clearing snow or renting the machine to neighbors. Or you can invest in a friend's business, trading money for a piece of the profits or some other benefit.

INVESTING IN OTHERS

Crowdfunding is a way for people to invest small sums in interesting projects and businesses. Websites such as Kickstarter.com allow people to contribute money to start-up projects such as making a film, starting a fashion company, or inventing a new app. Investors usually receive a gift of appreciation in return, which varies depending on the amount of the investment.

Don't put all your eggs in one basket! That old saying is a favorite to dust off when talking about investing. It means that you should not put all of your money in a single investment. Doing so is risky because if something happens to that investment, you could lose everything.

For example, you might really love hamburgers from a certain restaurant chain and decide to become part owner of that company by purchasing shares of its stock. But you wouldn't want to spend every penny you have on stock in this company. People may decide the burgers are unhealthy or don't taste good. Or the price of beef could skyrocket. That would hurt the restaurant and cause its stock price, and your investment, to decline in value.

The concept of putting your money in multiple types of investments is called diversification. To stick with the egg metaphor, diversification prevents all of your eggs from breaking if you stumble or the bottom falls out of a basket. With eggs spread out in several types of baskets, you take less risk and increase the chance that your money will be there for you, no matter what happens.

RISKY BUSINESS

Investments have various degrees of risk. Stock in a new company that is based overseas is riskier than money saved in a savings account at a bank. Taking greater risks can yield greater returns. But the losses can be greater as well.

Risk is not always about losing money. There is also the risk that money will grow too slowly to keep up with inflation or to reach your goals within your desired time frame.

We're used to a certain amount of risk in day-to-day life. How well each of us deals with risk depends on many factors. It's smart before deciding how to invest your money to figure out what's called your risk tolerance. There are many risk tolerance questionnaires you can try out online. One such quiz, developed by two university personal finance professors, asks such questions as:

You are on a TV game show and can choose one of the following. Which would you take?

$1,000 in cash

A 50% chance at winning $5,000

A 25% chance at winning $10,000

A 5% chance at winning $100,000

Suppose a relative left you an inheritance of $100,000, stipulating in the will that you invest ALL the money in ONE of the following choices. Which one would you select?

A savings account or money market mutual fund

A mutual fund that owns stocks and bonds

A portfolio of 15 common stocks

Commodities like gold, silver, and oil

Quiz source: http://njaes.rutgers.edu/money/riskquiz/

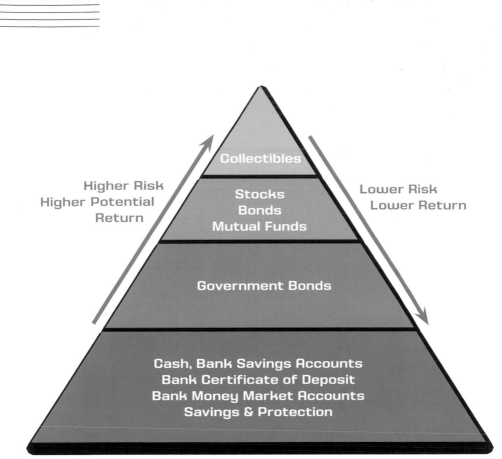

Higher Risk
Higher Potential
Return

Lower Risk
Lower Return

Collectibles

Stocks
Bonds
Mutual Funds

Government Bonds

Cash, Bank Savings Accounts
Bank Certificate of Deposit
Bank Money Market Accounts
Savings & Protection

Source: http://themint.org/kids/risk-and-rewards.html

REDUCE RISK

Investors can use diversification to reduce risk by varying the types of investments, such as stocks, bonds, cash, and property. When you'll need to access your money is also important so you won't need to take it out all at once.

It's hard to figure out what funds to set aside for the future without mapping what the future might bring. Like a road trip, you don't know exactly what you'll encounter along the way. There could be an accident, unexpected costs from a car breakdown, or the cost of a coffee needed for a jolt of energy. But part of planning is making educated guesses about what your life will look like and what financial needs you can estimate.

You'll need to figure out the right balance between saving, investing, spending, and donating. Finding this balance depends on your values, expenses, and goals.

Most experts suggest that if you have a retirement plan at your workplace, take advantage of it. Ideally, you'd be able to save 10 to 15 percent of your income. But if that's too much, at least save enough so that you qualify for any matching money your employer gives you. Typically, that's around 3 percent of your wages. Also save a small amount in an emergency savings fund. Experts suggest three to six months worth of bare-bones living expenses—think ramen noodles, not fancy restaurant meals. Or set a dollar-based goal, such as $10 per paycheck until you get to $100. Finally, think about opening a Roth IRA account, which is a great place to save for retirement because your money grows tax-free for life.

Both workplace retirement accounts and Roth IRAs give you incentives to save. If your employer contributes money to your workplace 401(k) plan provided you save a certain amount, that is an incentive.

The tax benefits of choosing to save in a workplace retirement plan, a Roth IRA account, or a 529 plan for college are incentives because the less money you owe the Internal Revenue Service, the more you get to keep. And it's important both at the individual level and for society as a whole to have people who are financially secure and prepared for whatever comes their way.

WHAT TO DO?

If you have a chunk of money, should you invest it all at once or over time? Depends. The argument for investing all at once is that the total amount of your money is fully invested for a longer period of time. The argument for investing a little bit at regular intervals is that you will invest at different price points. Because markets and investment prices fluctuate, if you purchase a bit at a time, it will balance out the points when you pay more or less for a share. That is sometimes referred to as buying high or low. This idea of investing a little at a time is called dollar-cost averaging. It is the common method for investing in workplace retirement plans.

GETTING ADVICE

Is your head spinning yet? Investing overwhelms many adults, so don't worry if it takes time to make sense of it all. Some people use a financial adviser to help them make financial decisions. Advisers go by various names—financial adviser, financial planner, broker, or wealth manager. Depending on their training and licensing, they may have special titles such as certified financial planner (CFP) or chartered life underwriter (CLU).

Financial advisers make investments and give financial advice, but they don't work for free. Some advisers earn a fee based on how much money they invest. Others earn commission based on the types of products they sell. You need to understand the fees you are charged for advice, because fees can take a big bite out of your return.

People don't typically start working with a financial adviser until their financial lives become more complicated and they have more money to invest. Many adults choose to manage their own financial affairs throughout life. It's common for teens to turn to people they know, such as their parents or guardians, for help with money matters. Websites and books can also help. But you need to understand the investments you are buying, even if you have someone knowledgeable helping you. Smart people have lost life savings to smooth-talking salespeople who have promised too-good-to-be-true returns from investments.

Supersized Stocks

If you invested some of your money in companies instead of spending it on the goods they make, you could make big bucks.

Share price in June 1999		Share price in June 2014
Apple	$ 1.64	$ 93.70
Disney	$24.08	$ 85.48
McDonald's	$29.79	$101.38
Nike	$12.37	$ 76.67

Source: http://finance.yahoo.com/stock-center/

MANAGING FEES

If you're not careful, you can be "fee'd" to death. OK, that's an overstatement, but fees do take a big bite out of your portfolio.

Assume that you are an employee with 35 years until retirement and a current 401(k) account balance of $25,000. If your returns during the next 35 years average 7 percent, and fees and expenses reduce your average returns by 0.5 percent, your account balance will grow to $227,000 at retirement, even if there are no further contributions to your account.

If fees and expenses are 1.5 percent, however, your account balance will reach only $163,000. The 1 percent difference in fees and expenses reduces your account balance at retirement by 28 percent.

Source: http://www.dol.gov/ebsa/publications/401k_employee.html

DOUBLE DOWN

Figuring out how long it will take for your investment to double is easier than you think, thanks to a mathematical rule named The Rule of 72. Here's the calculation:

Years to double = 72 divided by the interest rate (compounding annually)

For example, if you want your money to double in eight years, you need to earn an interest rate of 9 percent (8 equals 72 divided by 9). If you are earning 6 percent interest, it takes 12 years for your money to double.

The Stock Market Game

Are you curious about the stock market but lack funds to invest? The Stock Market Game gives you a virtual windfall of $100,000 to build a mock portfolio that you manage online. Schools usually sponsor the game, which lets you team up with friends to build your portfolio and market knowledge.

Other stock market simulators are available outside of school. Check out Wall Street Survivor online.

Here Today, Gone Tomorrow

If you were a kid years ago, you'd head to Woolworth's for the latest toy or school clothes. Wool-what? Exactly. There is risk in owning stock of a company. Even the seemingly most secure companies can be taken over by other companies or can file for bankruptcy. Nothing is forever, as this list of once-prominent companies shows. That's one reason why diversification is so important.

Woolworth's (1879–1997)
Montgomery Ward (1872–2000)
Pan Am Airlines (1927–1991)
Borders Books and Music (1971–2001)
Circuit City (1984–2009)

WHAT SHOULD I BUY?

We're confronted with decisions on how to spend our money every day. Some of the decisions seem small and unimportant. Should I buy flavored water or a soda? See a movie or buy a new video game?

Those small spending decisions add up to a lot of money over time and can make it difficult to afford bigger, more important purchases. Decisions about how we spend our money today also affect whether we'll have enough money to spend in the future.

Learning to make smart spending choices of all sizes is a critical life skill. So is choosing the right way to pay for purchases and how to be a savvy borrower.

CHAPTER SEVEN

SPENDING SMART

Money is a finite resource. There's only so much money available, and you have to make tough decisions about where your money goes. A good way to start is by understanding the difference between a need and a want. A need is an essential, a basic of life. Think food, water, shelter, electricity, and clothing.

Wants are items that are nice to have. Perhaps a tablet, a trip to the beach, new earrings, or an online subscription. Another term for wants is discretionary spending.

Sometimes there's a blurry line between needs and wants. Imagine you just got a new job. The office isn't within biking distance, and public transportation doesn't go in that direction. You will need a car to get to work. But what kind of car? You could look for an affordable used car that gets great gas mileage and is inexpensive to maintain. But it might not impress your friends. Or you could buy a more expensive new car that costs more to maintain, but it is exactly what you want. See? A car is a need, but the type of car you buy can veer into the want lane. This goes for clothing as well. You need jeans, sneakers, and T-shirts, but you don't need brand-name jeans, sneakers, or T-shirts.

Similarly, not everyone is going to have the same list of needs and wants. Some people will have items on their "need" list that are considered wants for others.

When you spend money, you give up the opportunity to do something else with it, such as save it or give it away. This is known as opportunity cost.

WANTS VS. NEEDS

How would you rate things in your own life?
Is each one a need or a want?

Item	Want	Need
Cell phone		
Car		
TV		
Smartphone		
Water		
House or apartment		
Energy drink		
Sneakers		
Exercise equipment		
Bed		
Microwave		

Net worth is the amount left when you subtract what you owe from what you own. What you own are your assets. What you owe are your liabilities. It's normal for teens and 20-somethings to have a low or even negative net worth, because debt for college, housing, or cars takes a bite out of whatever savings they might have.

PERSONAL NET WORTH WORKSHEET

Assets	Value
Checking accounts	$
Savings accounts	$
Money market accounts	$
Savings bonds	$
Certificates of deposit	$
401(k)	$
IRA	$
Roth IRA	$
Smartphone/computer/electronics	$
Car/bicycle/scooter	$
Home furnishings	$
Jewelry, art, collectibles	$
Total Assets	$

Liabilities	Amount Owed
Credit card balances	$
Estimated income tax owed	$
Other outstanding bills	$
Car loan	$
Student loans	$
Other long-term debt	$
Total Liabilities	$
NET WORTH (Assets minus Liabilities)	$

Another choice for spending your money is donating it to a charity. Americans give about $300 billion per year to charity. We give to feel good, support causes we feel connected to, and make the world a better place.

One incentive for adults to donate to charity is the tax break they receive for that donation, provided they itemize their tax deductions. This doesn't always apply to teens or young adults, but it's something to explore if you give a lot of money or goods to charity.

The United States has more than 1 million charities. Deciding how much to give and which organizations deserve your money is not an easy task. You can check with your local Better Business Bureau or visit websites that rate charities' financial and ethical performance, such as Charitynavigator.org, Guidestar.org, or Smartgivers.org.

Money is just one way to support a cause. If you're short on funds, consider giving your time instead. Teens in Kansas City can join the Greater Kansas City Community Foundation's Teen Giving Institute. They meet monthly to do hands-on work and learn about evaluating a charity for potential grants or funds. Do some research to see if there's a similar group in your area. Organizations from places of worship and schools regularly do volunteer work as well.

Another idea is to ask family and friends to donate money to a charity you support instead of giving you birthday or holiday gifts. Also, some of your stuff might be useful to charities. For example, animal rescue organizations can use old towels, child welfare organizations might like gently used toys, and charity-owned thrift stores could sell your cast-off clothing. If you have the ability and the desire to help, be creative, ask about needs in your area, and be willing to share your time and your strengths.

Ask yourself: Is this a need or a want? If it's a want, wait a little. Don't buy something the moment you see it. Think it over for a day or two. If you still want it, then make the trip to purchase it. Absence often eliminates desire.

Research before you buy. Make sure you are getting a good price for an item by doing some research before you make the purchase. Before the Internet you'd have to go from store to store or make phone calls to check prices and other product details. Today it's much easier to compare prices, on the Internet or by using a barcode reader price comparison app in stores. But price isn't the only important factor. It's smart to also evaluate the store's return policy and do research on the quality of the product. You may be better off spending a bit more for a higher quality product or one that comes with guarantees.

Look for ways to reduce costs. Do you get a discount for paying cash? Have you searched for a coupon? Is there a discount for buying in bulk? Will the price go down if you wait? It can be time-consuming, but asking for a way to save money is not being cheap. It's being frugal.

EMOTIONAL SPENDING

Money isn't just about numbers on a page or bills in a wallet. Emotion, desire, and others' opinions play a part in the financial decisions people make. For example, you might buy an expensive pair of shoes on impulse because you want to show them off to friends at a big party.

Scientists and economists who study money behavior work in the field of behavioral economics. This field has grown in importance in recent years.

How should people approach money knowing that emotions and irrational decisions can get in the way?

1. Awareness is a good first step.

2. Always step back or think twice before making big money decisions.

3. Create a spending plan and stick with it.

Daniel Kahneman, PhD, who won the Nobel Prize for economics in 2002 for his work with behavioral economics, has some advice: "Slow down, sleep on it, and ask your most brutal and least empathetic close friends for their advice."

BUDGETING

A budget is a road map for your money to follow. Without a map, you can easily get lost or overshoot your destination. Similarly, without a budget, you can easily lose sight of your financial goals, pay your bills late, or overspend. Many Americans spend more than they make, which is how they accumulate debt.

Creating a budget can be as high-tech or low-tech as you want. Either way, the basic process is the same. The first thing to do is figure out how much income you have. Base this on your net pay—the money you actually get in your paycheck after taxes and other deductions are withheld. Next catalog your fixed expenses, which are costs that are always there and stay the same. Rent, car and insurance payments, and monthly subscriptions are examples of fixed expenses. Then track your variable expenses, which are the costs that fluctuate. For example, money for utility bills, food, and entertainment are considered variable expenses. They can be needs or wants, and we make choices about how much to spend. While food is certainly a need, whether to dine on an inexpensive tuna sandwich or a pricey tuna sushi roll is your choice.

Most experts suggest keeping track of your spending for a month or two to understand your variable expenses. You can do this by writing each thing you buy in a notebook, by using your debit card for all transactions and combing through your bank statements, or by using a free personal financial management app like Mint.com. Apps are easier to use with debit or credit cards because using them creates a record of what you spend.

If you're eager to get started, you can use past bank statements as a start and try to estimate the rest. But often we're not so great at estimating true spending behavior in our heads.

Once you have numbers for fixed expenses and variable expenses, subtract those amounts from your income. Do you come up with a negative number? That means you are spending more than you earn. You'll need to make some decisions about cutting costs or finding ways to earn more money. Spending less than you make is one of the most important money principles to know. If you keep fixed expenses low and spend less than you make, you will have more financial flexibility and freedom.

SAMPLE BUDGET FOR TEENS

Category	Monthly Budget	Actual Amount	Difference
INCOME:	**Estimate Your Income**	**Your Actual Income**	
Wages/Income Paycheck, Allowance, Birthday Money, etc.	$200	$210	$10
Interest Income From Savings Account	$5	$4	($1)
INCOME SUBTOTAL	$205	$214	$9
EXPENSES:	**Estimate Your Expenses**	**Your Actual Expenses**	
Savings			
Savings Account	$10	$10	$0
Bills			
Taxes—from Paycheck	$30	$32	($2)
Rent/Mortgage	$0	$0	$0
Utilities—Electricity, Cell Phone, etc.	$30	$30	$0
Groceries/Snacks	$15	$12	$3
Car			
Car Payment	$0	$0	$0
Car Insurance	$0	$0	$0
Gasoline	$20	$25	($5)
Shopping			
Clothes	$40	$35	$5
Other Shopping	$10	$0	$10
Fun			
Entertainment— Movies, Video Games, Pizza, Bowling, etc.	$20	$25	($5)
Other Expenses	Ski Club: $10	Ski Club: $10	$0
EXPENSES SUBTOTAL	**$185**	**$179**	**$6**
NET INCOME	**$20**	**$35**	**$15**

Source: http://www.moneyandstuff.info/pdfs/SampleBudgetforTeens.pdf

Do you have money left over? This is a good place to be. But you're not finished!

The next step is to look at where your money has been going and ask yourself if you're using your money the way you want. Are you saving for important goals such as college or a car? Do you have enough savings in case you want to go on a school trip? If not, it's time to tweak your budget so your money reflects your goals and values.

Remember money is just a tool that helps you live the life you want. Your budget is a road map for getting there. No one gets a budget right the first time, and your budget will need to shift as your life changes.

During your budget building, it's likely that you thought about your life and what's important to you. This will come in handy for prioritizing your spending. For most of us, money runs out before all of our goals and dreams are met. This means we have to make decisions about what to do with our money first.

Here are some guidelines to follow

- **Pay yourself first.** Find a way to save a little bit of money, even if it's just a few dollars. Set this aside before you do anything else. Ideally, you'll have the resources to save for multiple goals—emergency savings, retirement, and fun stuff such as vacations, a car, or a new TV.

- **Take care of yourself next.** You need food, shelter, and medical care. Be mindful of what you spend because the costs vary wildly.

- **Fixed big-ticket expenses come next.** Rent, car payments, insurance, debt payments, and college bills fall into this category.

- **List wants.** They could include monthly subscriptions, movies, trips, and other items and experiences that make life fun. If money is tight, you shouldn't rank these expenses above your bills and future goals.

There are so many ways to pay
the purchases you make. Here's
rundown, including the pros
cons of each method.

CASH

PROS

- Accepted everywhere. Even some other countries accept U.S. dollars.

- Tangible. Some experts say people think more about cash purchases because they see the money leaving their hands and notice when it runs out.

- No worries about debt. You can't spend more cash than you have.

CONS

- To get cash, you must visit your bank or find an ATM. ATMs are nearly everywhere, but your bank might not have a machine located where you need to withdraw money. Using another bank's ATM often involves a fee, and your bank may also charge you a fee on top of that.

- Cash that's lost or stolen cannot be replaced.

BALANCING ACT

If you have a checking account with a traditional bank, odds are you received a checkbook when you opened your account. Odds are also good that you haven't thought about your checkbook since and might not even know where it is. With forms of payment such as debit and credit cards, many checkbooks have been relegated to the back of the desk drawer. Fewer businesses even accept checks these days.

So when you hear the phrase "balancing a checkbook," you might think it doesn't apply to you. But it's essentially the equivalent of online budgeting or account management. It means writing down what you've spent and subtracting it from the total in your account, so you don't spend more than you have. Balancing your checkbook also allows you to compare what the bank says you've deposited and spent with what you think you've done, just in case there are errors.

Credit means using money you've borrowed from a bank to make purchases today, with the intention of paying back the bank at a specific time. Credit cards are essentially short-term loans.

PROS

- Instant gratification and convenience. You don't have to wait to buy a good or service until you have the money.

- Tracking. Credit card statements provide a nice monthly record of how much you spend.

- Rewards. Some banks issue rewards when you use their credit cards to buy things. The rewards can be redeemed for items such as airline tickets, merchandise or gift cards, or cash back.

- Credit history. If you manage your credit card account well, the history will help qualify you for more favorable terms for mortgages and car loans.

CONS

- Too convenient. Credit makes it easy to overspend.

- Interest. Banks charge interest for borrowing money with credit cards, unless you pay it back within the grace period. This means you are ultimately paying more for the items you purchased, reducing the amount of money for buying other things or saving.

- Access. Not everyone has access to or qualifies for credit cards.

- Acceptance. Not all stores accept credit cards because store owners have to pay fees to credit card issuers.

- Teens who apply for a credit card may need a co-signer. A co-signer—an adult who agrees to have his or her name on the credit card account as well—is liable for any money owed if the primary borrower stops paying the debt.

DEBIT CARDS

A plastic payment card issued by your bank that lets you access the money in your account.

PROS

- Accepted nearly everywhere.

- Convenient. Debit cards offer the convenience of credit without worrying about racking up a big bill.

- Fast. No counting out change or scribbling a check.

- Easier to get than credit cards. Most bank accounts now come with debit cards.

- Good for tracking. Debit cards provide a record of what you spent, which makes budgeting easier.

. . . .

CONS

- Fees. If you spend more than you have in your account, you could be charged expensive overdraft fees, unless you link your debit card to a credit card or other account that covers deficits.

- Fraud. Credit cards have more protection than debit cards in cases of liability and fraud. If you don't report your lost or misused debit card quickly, you could be liable for up to $500 of purchases you didn't make. Plus your money can be tied up during the investigation.

- Buying with debit cards doesn't help build your credit history.

- Rewards for using a debit card are rare in the current banking environment.

Bitcoin

There are many ways to pay for things. Cash, credit, even on your phone. But a new method of payment is very different from any of those because it's not based on the U.S. dollar or any other country's currency. It's called bitcoin and is a virtual online currency that can be used to buy goods and services at a limited but growing number of stores and websites. Two young girls in San Francisco even accept bitcoin at their cookie stand.

Powerful computers must "mine" for bitcoins by solving complex math problems, but you can also purchase the "cryptocurrency" on exchanges. Not everyone has heard of bitcoin, but the currency has grown in notoriety as the value has fluctuated greatly, and one bitcoin exchange claims to have lost hundreds of thousands of bitcoins.

PREPAID CARDS AND GIFT CARDS

These cards look and work much like debit cards, but they are purchased at a store with cash, credit, or a debit card. Some can only be used at certain stores. Others can be used anywhere and reloaded with funds when the money runs out.

PROS

- Convenience of plastic without the worries that come with credit cards or the need for a bank account.

- Available to anyone, regardless of his or her credit history.

- Good for managing a budget. You can carry a certain card for each kind of purchase to help keep your budget in check.

. . . .

CONS

- May have complex terms and conditions. Prepaid cards you can use anywhere are less regulated than debit and credit cards, so it's even more critical that you understand the rules involved. Gift cards for use at specific stores and restaurants have more consumer protections.

- Fees. Using some prepaid cards incurs fees for nearly everything, from checking your balance to loading new funds.

- Protection. Unlike money in the bank, prepaid cards aren't always covered by FDIC insurance.

- Stores can go out of business before you use a gift card, making it difficult, if not impossible, to get your money back.

BARTERING

Trading goods or services with others is a way to get what you need or want without using money or credit.

PROS

- Easy on the bank account. You can get something without having to save.

- Easy on the Earth. Trading items you no longer have use for is better for the environment than throwing them away.

. . . .

CONS

- No protection. If the other person doesn't fulfill his or her end of the bargain, or you find the items or service are misrepresented, there's little you can do.

- Limited options. It may not always be possible to barter what you have for what you need.

SAVING IS GOOD ENOUGH FOR A RAPPER

Bling. Mansions. Pricey cars. Think of the lifestyle portrayed by rap artists, and these images of luxury probably come to mind. Money—earning and spending loads of it—is a recurring theme in rap music. But a rap song that reached No. 1 on the Billboard top 100 chart in 2013 sends a different message. Macklemore and Lewis' "Thrift Shop" explores themes of buying secondhand and saving money, as Macklemore explains in this interview with MTV:

"Rappers talk about, oh I buy this and I buy that, and I spend this much money and I make it rain, and this type of champagne and painting the club, and this is the kind of record that's the exact opposite. It's the polar opposite of it. It's kind of standing for like let's save some money, let's keep some money away, let's spend as little as possible and look as fresh as possible at the same time."

Macklemore

CHAPTER EIGHT

BRILLIANT BORROWING

If you're in need of cash, one option is to borrow it. But borrowing is a major decision. You don't want to end up taking on more debt than you can safely pay back.

You might have heard the term "financing." That means taking out a loan to purchase a big-ticket item, such as a car, house, or furniture. Young people also commonly borrow money to pay for college. And when you pay for purchases with a credit card, you are using the bank's money and agreeing to pay it back. If you buy a candy bar with a credit card, you are borrowing money to pay for it.

You have several options if you decide to get a loan. You can ask family or friends for a loan. You can borrow from a bank, either through a credit card or a bank loan. It tends to be easier to qualify for a credit card than for a bank loan. Since the Great Recession of 2007–2009, banks have stricter loan standards.

Peer-to-peer lending websites such as lendingclub.com and prosper.com are another option. These sites allow strangers to lend and borrow money from one another.

COSTS OF BORROWING

Banks lend money to make money. When you borrow from a bank, the bank charges you interest. You must pay the interest back along with the amount you originally borrowed, which is called the principal. However, if you borrow money from friends and family, they might not charge you interest.

Whether to borrow from family and friends can be a sensitive issue, so it's important to devise a clear plan for how to pay it back or you risk straining your personal relationships.

When you borrow money for a house or car, the lender will usually require a down payment up front. It's calculated based on the total purchase price of the item. A typical down payment is 20 percent of the purchase price, but smaller and larger down payments also may be allowed.

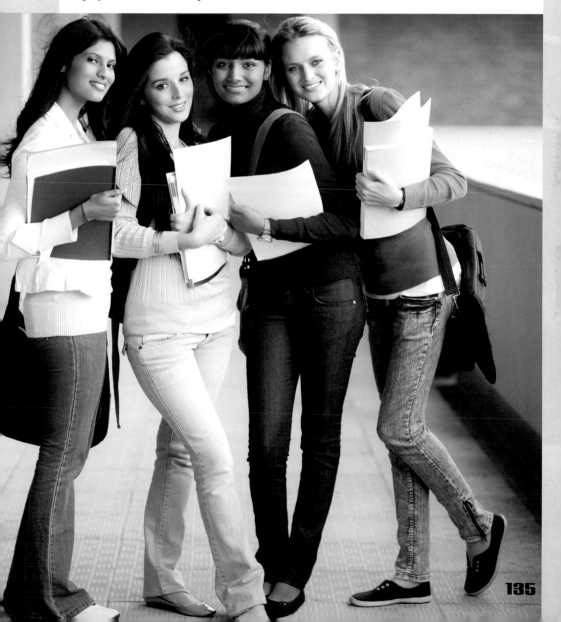

At one time it was very easy to get a credit card. Companies even used to market credit cards on college campuses, offering students free T-shirts and other goodies in exchange for filling out a credit application. The widespread availability of credit got some teens and young adults in trouble. And stories about how credit contributed to the financial problems of the Great Recession have some consumers fearing credit cards.

But credit isn't all bad. It's a way to make purchases easily without having to carry a lot of cash. Credit creates a helpful record of your spending and is a good safety net if you need money in a crunch. But the terms and conditions of credit cards, which often are buried in fine print, must be understood so you don't spend more than you can afford to repay or rack up unexpected interest and fees.

A good rule is to use a credit card for just the purchases that you can afford to pay off within the grace period, which is the amount of time you have to pay your credit card bill before you are charged interest. Interest on credit cards is measured with an annual percentage rate (APR), which means interest expressed over a yearlong period. The grace period usually is about a month, but check with your credit card company to be sure.

WOULD YOU LIKE A CREDIT CARD WITH YOUR T-SHIRT?

Credit card companies are restricted by law from marketing cards the way they used to. If you're younger than 21, you must prove you have the income to pay your bill or have a co-signer who is older than 21 who agrees to pay if you can't. Another way to build credit is to have a parent add you as an authorized user to his or her credit card account.

Most banks require a minimum monthly payment on credit card accounts. Minimum payments tend to be small—as little as 2 to 3 percent of your total balance. But don't be tempted to pay only the minimum. The less you pay on your bill, the more you'll end up paying in the long run. If, for example, you have $1,000 in debt at an APR of 18 percent and your minimum payment is 2 percent, you'll pay a total of $1,863—$863 in interest—and take eight years to pay off the bill. If you doubled the minimum, you'd pay the debt in three years and save $600 in interest. If you don't have the money to pay your credit card bill in full, pay off as much as possible to limit the amount of interest you're charged.

this card and each month you pay ...

Only the minimum payment

If you would like information about credit counseling services, refer to www

1-877-285-2108.

ortant Information

WHETHER YOU

payment e.

You will pay off the this statem

3

Credit card companies are now required by law to include a section on the minimum payment on cardholders' monthly statements. The section should include how long it will take to pay off the bill at the minimum monthly payment, as well as the total amount charged.

In addition to minimums, there are also maximums. Cards have a credit limit, which is the maximum amount you can have on your credit card account at one time. Keep in mind that banks can set credit limits pretty high. Limits are no indication that you should charge that amount of money or could even afford to pay off that much debt.

Interest is just one type of fee banks may charge for credit card use. There are late payment fees, fees for using the card at ATMs, and fees for transferring charges you have on one card to another. Some banks also charge an annual fee for cards. These cards typically come with travel rewards or other benefits. It's important to calculate whether it makes sense to pay an annual fee for a credit card. In most cases the answer will be no, especially if it's your first credit card or you carry a balance. Cards that give users rewards tend to have higher interest rates.

...e, you may have to pay a late fee up to $35.

period, you will pay more in interest and it will take you longer to pay off

w Balance shown on in about ...	And you will end up paying an estimated total of ...
rs	
sdoj.gov/ust/eo/bapcpa/ccde/cc ann...	$517

Perks in the *Fine* Print

The fine print of credit card agreements is riddled with legal terms and hidden fees. But it also can contain perks that people may overlook.

PRICEY PIZZAS

It's Friday night and you're out with friends. You decide to go out for pizza. You are trying to be a savvy spender, so you buy the pizza special—$2 off a large pepperoni. You charge the $15 cost to your credit card. Your friends give you cash for their share, so your true cost was just $5. But you end up spending the $10 on candy and chips at the convenience store.

Let's say this scenario plays out each Friday. After about a year you find yourself with a $750 credit card bill and only enough money to pay $20 a month. If your credit card charges an interest rate of 18 percent, it will take five years to pay for those large pies, and you'll pay an extra $361 in interest. It's a calculation that can give you massive indigestion, especially when you think about how that money could have paid for a new smartphone or other big purchase.

Three key perks of some credit cards
- Fraud protection: If your card is used without your permission, the law states you are not liable for more than $50 of the charges. Many major banks have zero liability policies for lost or stolen cards.
- Extended warranties: Some banks add more time to the warranty for items purchased with the card.
- Purchase protection: If you buy an item that is stolen or breaks right away, your bank might pay to replace it.

Your credit score is kind of like a grade-point average for your money life. It's used by banks to decide whether to lend you money and at what interest rate. But landlords and insurance agents also look at it when deciding whether to rent you an apartment or to determine your car insurance costs. If your score is in the basement, you could lose out.

There are several credit scores on the market, but most lenders look at the FICO score, which is named for the score's creator, the Fair Isaac Corporation. The score ranges vary, but the higher the score, the better. Some credit card issuers provide a free peek at your credit score. If they don't, you can purchase a score for less than $20 at MyFico.com or estimate your score for free at creditkarma.com.

Your credit score is based on your credit report. This document is filled with your financial history—which accounts you have and how well you've managed them. You have the right to receive one free credit report from each of the three major credit bureaus every year through www.annualcreditreport.com. You should take advantage of that free report not only to check for mistakes, but also to check for identity theft or other types of fraud.

1. **Keep your balance low in relation to your available credit.**

Keeping your credit balance to 25 percent or below your available credit is a good general rule. But don't open credit accounts you don't intend to use just to improve this ratio.

2. **Pay your bills on time.**

3. **Make more than the minimum payment.**

4. **Don't open a lot of new accounts over a short period of time.**

Having many inquiries into your credit report and expanding your available credit too quickly may signal to creditors that you're on the brink of major financial problems.

5. **Review your credit report regularly and correct errors.**

You can easily get your credit report online. Visit www.annualcreditreport.com and follow the instructions for correcting credit report errors with the credit bureaus.

Source: http://whatsmyscore.org/facts/

If you're having trouble qualifying for a credit card because you have no history or a low credit score, a secured credit card is one option.

A secured credit card requires you to deposit money in an account before making purchases. An unsecured credit card doesn't require any money up front. The bank is placing faith in you to pay back the charges.

BUYING YOUR RIDE

For many teens, buying a car is their first major purchase. When you buy your first car, you'll need all of your financial literacy skills—assessing needs versus wants; researching a big purchase; budgeting for the car payment, gas, insurance, and maintenance; and using savings or getting financing. They are all important when it comes to selecting the right vehicle for the right price.

CHAPTER NINE

PAYING FOR COLLEGE

For many teens, college is the biggest expense of their lives so far. Fortunately, there is a lot of financial assistance available for getting that degree.

Most people can't afford to just pay for college. You would have to be quite wealthy to cover six figures' worth of college costs without blinking an eye. That's why it's important to understand all of the tools out there to help you.

Planning for college costs should start long before you head to campus. Some parents start saving before their kids are born! But even if you are in your last year of high school, it's better late than never. Online calculators can help you figure out your estimated family contribution for college, based on income and other factors.

When you are in high school, you and your family should fill out the Free Application for Federal Student Aid (FAFSA). This is the starting point for determining your eligibility for loans, work-study, and other programs created to help students pay for college. Fill it out even if you think your parents have too much money to receive aid.

What It Costs

$18,391. That's the average cost of a year's in-state tuition, fees, and room and board for a public college in 2013-14. The cost more than doubles for private schools. The main costs you should budget for include:

- **Tuition and fees**

- **Room and board: The cost of your dorm room or apartment and cafeteria plan**

- **Books and supplies**

- **Spending money: The cost of things such as late-night pizzas, cell phone bills, clothes, and laundry. These costs vary, and many students are surprised by how quickly they add up.**

- **Transportation: The cost of your bus pass, bike, or car**

Let's take a look at the main tools available to pay for college:

Savings: Money saved in a regular savings account or a 529 plan, which is an account dedicated to college costs.

Available cash: Money set aside from your or your parents' paycheck to cover college costs.

Financial aid: A broad term used to describe loans and grants given to a student from the school and the government to pay for college. Many types of financial aid are available from the federal government and private organizations. After you are accepted, your college will send you a financial aid letter detailing a proposal for how you'll pay for college. The most important thing to keep in mind is that financial aid is not necessarily free money. It often includes loans you must pay back. The key pieces of financial aid are grants, scholarships, and loans.

You're In!

Once you receive your college acceptances, it's time to decipher your financial aid award letters. Your high school guidance counselor should be able to help you, and you can find many resources on the Internet. The college's financial aid office can also answer your questions. As with any financial decision, you must understand every piece of a financial aid offer and how it compares with other offers you've received. You don't want any big dollar surprises as you set out on your own.

GRANTS AND SCHOLARSHIPS

Neither grants nor scholarships need to be paid back. Scholarships tend to be awarded based on merit, such as earning good grades, writing a great essay, or doing well in a particular activity. Colleges, private organizations, and even your parents' employers may give scholarships. You can research many scholarships online. Just remember that legitimate scholarships do not require up-front fees. Your high school guidance counselor can help you find and apply for legitimate scholarships.

Grants tend to be awarded on the basis of financial need. Many college students receive Pell Grants from the federal government. Colleges give need-based aid as well, which allows some lower-income students to afford expensive private colleges.

LOANS

The federal government offers college loans. If you have financial need, you'll qualify for a subsidized loan—a loan that does not accumulate interest while you're in school. Other federal loans include unsubsidized loans, which do accumulate interest during your studies. The federal government also offers loans to parents called PLUS loans.

Banks offer college loans, but be careful to read the fine print. These loans tend to have less favorable terms than government loans and often require a co-signer, such as your parent or guardian.

In addition, you can charge college expenses on a credit card. However, that isn't a recommended way to pay for college.

Researching and applying for college is filled with daydreaming, excitement, and possibility. Where will you go? What will you major in? What will your career be? A question that isn't always on that list but should be: How much can I afford to borrow?

It's a tough question to answer because there are so many unknowns about where college will take you and what career you'll ultimately have. But it's critical to explore some scenarios so you don't end up with crippling debt. College debt is nearly impossible to get rid of through bankruptcy. Debt forgiveness programs for federal loans don't start until you've been paying the debt for a decade or more in most cases. One strategy is to check out debt repayment calculators online, such as http://mappingyourfuture.org/paying/debtwizard. Or listen to an expert's opinion. "The total amount of student debt should not exceed the borrower's anticipated annual salary for the first year out of school," says Allesandra Lanza of the nonprofit organization American Student Assistance.

TIPS TO MINIMIZE THE COST OF COLLEGE

1. Work part-time
2. Earn college credits in high school
3. Live at home
4. Buy used textbooks or rent your books
5. Graduate on time

Expert Advice on Saving for College

Kathy Ruby, a college finance consultant at getintocollege.com and a former financial aid director at St. Olaf College in Minnesota, has advice for would-be college students:

Talk to your parents or guardians.

Find out what they can afford and are willing to pay for your college education. It's not always an easy conversation (for them or for you), but it's one that you need to have.

Read your e-mail. Every day.

Colleges expect you to; it is how they will communicate with you about important things like required health forms, financial aid applications, and, of course, paying your bill. Unlike high school, colleges e-mail you, not your parents. Learn to manage your e-mail account: Sort e-mails you need to keep into folders, respond in a timely manner, and delete the ones you don't need. Unsubscribe yourself from advertiser mailing lists. In other words, avoid having 1,697 e-mails in your inbox.

Pay attention to deadlines. They

matter. Especially when it comes to getting money for college. Every college will have deadlines listed clearly on its Financial Aid Office website. And don't let the forms intimidate you. They are simpler than they look and can really pay off. Let's say it takes you three hours to complete the FAFSA, and, as a result, you are awarded a $3,000 grant. When was the last time you got paid $1,000 an hour, tax-free?

PROTECT YOURSELF!

Do you remember the first time you lost something that was important to you? Say you were 5 and took your brand-new change purse or pencil case to school. At the end of the school day, it was nowhere to be found. You can probably still remember the feeling of loss that enveloped you when you realized that your prized possession was gone forever. Some losses can't be prevented. But there are ways to prepare for others. Being able to handle loss when it happens is one reason to plan and save. Another way to protect yourself is to buy insurance. Some types of policies make more sense for a young adult to have than others. Not sure how they work? There are several types of policies, but they all work to protect you or your possessions. And what about protecting your identity? Identity theft can be worse than a car theft or a break-in at your house. There are several steps you can take to protect yourself from becoming an identity theft victim.

CHAPTER TEN

THE BASICS:
RISK AND INSURANCE

Without risk, there would be no need for insurance. Risk—the possibility that something bad will happen—is all around us, all the time.

It is impossible to erase risk from our lives. But there are ways to deal with it. You can:

- *Steer clear of risk.* **Some risks can be avoided altogether. For example, you can choose never to smoke cigarettes or accept a ride from someone who has been drinking alcohol.**

- *Reduce risk.* **It is possible to reduce the risk that bad things will happen. For example, you can wear a helmet when riding your bike, or leave lights on a timer each time you go on vacation to deter burglars.**

- *Share risk.* **This is what you are doing when you purchase insurance. You are spreading out the risk so if something bad happens, you won't have to handle it all by yourself.**

Do you remember a time when you were taking a risk that made you feel uncomfortable? Maybe your palms were sweaty or you were sick to your stomach. Maybe you couldn't concentrate on anything else or found your mind racing to the worst-case scenario.

Various people have various risk tolerance levels. If you were about to cross the Grand Canyon on a high wire, you'd probably have all of the symptoms described above and then some. But daredevil Nik Wallenda, who has been walking on a wire since he was 2, would assess the risk of walking on a steel cable high above the Colorado River differently. In June 2013 he took just less than 23 minutes to successfully complete this incredibly risky stunt.

Nik Wallenda crossing the Grand Canyon

Risk tolerance also varies by situation. You may not be able to walk a high wire, but you might be comfortable with the risk of injury when playing your favorite sport or the risk of losing money in the stock market.

THE YOUNG AND THE RISKY

Scientists have learned that the frontal cortex—the part of the brain in charge of impulse control, judging risk, and making decisions—isn't fully developed until a person is 25 years old. This is one reason car insurance costs more for teens and young adults. Unmarried men who are younger than 25 pay the most for car insurance.

WHAT IS INSURANCE?

Insurance is designed to protect you and your finances when something unfortunate and unexpected takes place. Its purpose is to mitigate (lessen) the risk. When you buy an insurance policy, you're basically buying a contract that says if certain adverse things happen, the insurance company will cover agreed-upon costs for you, the policyholder. The contract explains what the insurance will and won't cover. For example, health insurance won't cover every medical procedure, and car insurance won't cover every breakdown. Yet these policies will cover the major mishaps that could wipe out your savings or your parents' or guardians' savings.

There are many types of insurance—too many to list here. But the basic types of insurance cover people, such as yourself or your family, or property, including your car, home, or personal belongings. Life, disability, and health insurance fall in the first group. Car insurance and homeowners or renters insurance fall in the second. You can even purchase small insurance policies for your smartphone or to refund your airfare in case you have to cancel a vacation.

Insurance policies vary in price, based on many factors. For example, living in an area with a higher crime rate will result in more expensive renters insurance. Driving a sports car or simply being a new driver will cause higher car insurance rates. Smoking cigarettes will lead to costlier life insurance.

No one likes to think of paying for something he or she will never use. But some risks are too costly to cover on your own. When choosing whether to buy insurance, you need to ask yourself if you could afford to pay the costs of a health or property emergency up front. If the answer is no, you'd better buy insurance. If the answer is yes, then you need to set enough money aside in a savings account to cover any potential losses. Otherwise a loss could blindside you.

Deciding whether to purchase insurance is up to you—to some degree. For example, you must have health insurance or face a penalty. And you are required to have auto insurance in most states, but no one will force you to buy insurance for your smartphone.

WHERE TO BUY

You can buy insurance online, through a site that collects information from multiple insurance companies to make it easier to compare policies and prices. Or you can buy directly from an insurer's website or mobile app. You also can buy insurance through an insurance agent, who will help determine the right policy for you and take care of the paperwork. Some agents are independent, meaning they can sell policies from more than one insurance company. Others are captive agents, selling policies from only one company. You will have more choices with an independent agent. Insurance agents make their money through commissions earned from the company selling the policy.

Whether you choose a website or an agent for insurance shopping, you'll receive an estimated price called a quote for the type of policy you're considering, based on information you've given them about yourself and your insurance needs. If you choose to buy the insurance policy, your cost is called a premium.

If you ever need to use an insurance policy, known as making a claim, you will usually pay a deductible. This amount is what you are responsible to pay before the insurance company will make a payout. Deductibles vary in amount. Generally, the higher the deductible, the lower the premium. Always set aside enough money in a savings account to pay your deductible so that your deductible doesn't become debt.

PAYMENT OPTIONS

You'll usually have several options for paying your insurance premiums. You often have the choice to pay monthly, quarterly, or annually. Sometimes paying a lump sum instead of monthly payments will net you a decent discount. You can have the money automatically withdrawn from your bank account or be billed for the premium. If you receive health insurance through an employer, your premium will be deducted from your paycheck. Homeowners often automatically pay their house insurance along with their mortgage payment from what's called an escrow account.

If you forget to pay your premium or don't have the funds to cover it, most insurers will give you about 30 days to pay before canceling your policy. Letting your insurance policy lapse is a pain. If it's a life insurance policy, you may have to go through another health examination and could end up paying more for your policy.

If the policy is for auto insurance, the consequences are even more serious. A lapse of even one day could raise your rate once you buy a new policy, because uninsured drivers are considered higher risk. Not only that, but driving without at least liability insurance is illegal in every state but New Hampshire. And if you have a car loan, you are required to have insurance. If you don't buy your own policy, the lender will buy a policy for you at a very steep rate. In an extreme case, the lender might repossess your wheels.

If you take out a loan to buy a home, you'll also need insurance. Mortgage holders require homeowners to have insurance and will purchase extremely expensive insurance for the homeowner if the situation isn't corrected right away. For those with renters insurance, if your policy lapses and the rental unit experiences a fire or other disaster, you're out not only the cost of a policy you never used, but also the replacement cost of every one of your possessions.

KNOW THE SCORE

Before an insurance company decides whether to offer you an insurance policy and at what premium, the company assesses how risky it will be to insure you. There are many ways that the insurance company will assess a potential customer's risk. It will look at past behavior—have you been in previous car accidents, do you lose a lot of items, or are you known to jump out of airplanes? It will take into consideration what you are insuring and where. For example, a sports car in a city with a high crime rate will typically cost a lot more to insure than a minivan in the suburbs.

An insurer will also look at your financial behavior, particularly how you handle credit. Insurers have found that a person's credit behavior can predict how likely it is for that person to have an insurance loss. Some states have restrictions on how credit-based insurance scores are used. But the bottom line is that the way you handle credit can affect other areas of your life, so it is important to use credit responsibly.

KEEPING AHEAD OF CHANGE

Life changes a lot when you're young. Think of all the scenarios. You might buy a car, move to a different state, switch jobs, or get married. Each time your life changes, you'll need to look at whether your insurance needs have changed as well.

Even in years when you don't have a major life event, it pays to reevaluate your policies. Premiums fluctuate based on market conditions and can go down. As you get older and exhibit responsible behavior such as paying your premium on time, you may be offered a lower premium. Check your policy and its premium every couple of years.

DO I REALLY NEED IT?

You might wonder if you really need to worry about insurance. After all, you're just a teen—you probably don't have much to protect. And some of the insurance policies your parents have will protect you as well. For example, federal law requires health care companies to allow young adults to stay on their parents' policy until they turn 26, even if they are married and financially independent.

If you're living at home, you can stay on your parents' car insurance as well, regardless of how old you are. Usually you can stay on your parents' policy when you're in college too, because your dorm room is not considered your permanent residence.

Sometimes your parents' homeowners insurance policy will also cover your belongings at college. Be sure to have them contact their agent or read the details of their policy. Otherwise you should find the money in your budget to buy a renters insurance policy, even in a dorm room. Bottom line, you should always have health insurance, disability insurance, renters or homeowners insurance, and auto insurance, whether it's your parents' policy or your own.

KEEPING IT SOCIAL

Social media can be a great way to keep in touch with the companies that have your business. The companies' Facebook pages and Twitter feeds can contain a lot of valuable and entertaining information. But you should be careful about the types of posts and photos you place on your social media pages. What you share via social media could be considered by insurance companies when evaluating your policy or examining a claim.

CHAPTER ELEVEN

PROTECTING YOUR STUFF

Buying a car is a big deal. You have to save for a long time, research which car to buy, and find the right vehicle. Then the moment comes, and you get to slide behind the wheel. It's an exciting moment. But it's also a little nerve-wracking. What if something goes wrong? That's what insurance is for.

If an accident happens, car insurance can help pay for:

- *Damage to your car*

- *Damage you cause in an accident*

- *Medical bills for injuries from a car accident*

- *Damage caused by a noninsured driver. Even though most states require car insurance, not every driver purchases it.*

Car insurance includes several components. Some are optional and some aren't. The requirements vary by state. Scrimping on insurance can be risky, and often adding a little more coverage doesn't cost that much more. An insurance agent or quick web search on insurance minimums in your state can help you start thinking about how much insurance to buy.

There are six parts to basic auto insurance:

- *Bodily injury liability pays for injuries you cause to someone else, whether you're driving your own car or someone else's with their permission.*

- *Personal injury protection pays for your injuries and the injuries of your passengers. It also helps cover lost wages in case you can't immediately return to work.*

- *Property damage liability pays for damage you cause to another person's car or property.*

- *Collision pays for damage to your car, whether it's a fender bender or a car-crushing crash, and regardless of whose fault it is. The insurance company will pay to get your car fixed, or give you a certain amount toward a new car if your old car is totaled.*

- *Comprehensive covers damage or loss of your vehicle that's not caused in a crash. For example, if a tree branch falls on your car, comprehensive kicks in. If your car is stolen, comprehensive pays. Older cars might need less or no comprehensive insurance. It depends on how much your car is worth and whether you have savings to pay for a new one if needed.*

- *Underinsured and uninsured coverage kicks in if you're involved in a hit-and-run accident or an accident involving an uninsured driver.*

Homeowners insurance covers the cost of rebuilding your house and replacing the belongings inside in the event of a fire or other disaster. Renters insurance covers the loss of personal property inside a rented home or apartment. Your parents' homeowners insurance may cover your personal belongings, even if you are attending college and living away from home. If that's not the case, strongly consider a renters insurance policy. You may think you don't own much of value. But if you own a few electronic devices, a closetful of clothes, and a few pieces of furniture, odds are you couldn't afford to replace them all without wiping out most or all of your savings.

To gauge how much your possessions are worth, do a home inventory. You can walk around your bedroom, house, or apartment and write down your belongings, with an estimate of what amount they're worth. Taking a video and storing it in a safe-deposit box, the cloud, or other secure location is also a helpful way to inventory your stuff.

Remember that insurance isn't just for large items such as cars and TVs. For example, you can insure your smartphone or tablet. If you lose your smartphone, it's reasonable to consider buying another one with your savings or downgrading to a basic phone until you can afford a better one. It's also reasonable to pay $10 a month for insurance that will replace your phone if you drop it. What you decide depends on many factors, but mostly your risk tolerance.

Teen Inventory

Item	Replacement Value
TV	
Game System	
Computer	
Tablet	
Phone	
Bed	
Bureau/Dresser	
Desk	
Clothes	
Shoes	
Books	
Jewelry	

Where you live also affects your auto insurance premium. You can use carinsurance.com's "Be Nosy" calculator to see how insurance rates fluctuate by ZIP code.

2014 STATE RANKINGS OF CAR INSURANCE RATES

* Dollar figures shown are an average of insurance rates for all 855 vehicles surveyed in the 2014 model year.

Rank	State	Avg. annual premium*	Rank	State	Avg. annual premium*
1	Michigan	$ 2,551	26	Hawaii	$ 1,400
2	West Virginia	$ 2,518	27	Arkansas	$ 1,399
3	Georgia	$ 2,201	28	Tennessee	$ 1,397
4	Washington, D.C.	$ 2,127	29	Nevada	$ 1,388
5	Rhode Island	$ 2,020	30	Mississippi	$ 1,385
6	Montana	$ 2,013	31	New Mexico	$ 1,371
7	Louisiana	$ 1,971	32	Illinois	$ 1,370
8	California	$ 1,962	33	Minnesota	$ 1,360
9	New Jersey	$ 1,905	34	Kansas	$ 1,358
10	Florida	$ 1,830	35	Oregon	$ 1,333
11	Maryland	$ 1,810	36	Nebraska	$ 1,317
12	North Dakota	$ 1,710	37	South Carolina	$ 1,316
13	Connecticut	$ 1,638	38	Arizona	$ 1,222
14	Texas	$ 1,620	39	Missouri	$ 1,207
15	Alaska	$ 1,605	40	Indiana	$ 1,202
16	Massachusetts	$ 1,604	41	Utah	$ 1,192
17	Delaware	$ 1,580	42	New York	$ 1,173
18	Oklahoma	$ 1,568	43	Vermont	$ 1,149
19	Colorado	$ 1,558	44	Virginia	$ 1,114
20	South Dakota	$ 1,557	45	Wisconsin	$ 1,087
21	Wyoming	$ 1,541	46	North Carolina	$ 1,060
22	Alabama	$ 1,529	47	Iowa	$ 1,058
	National average	$ 1,503	48	Idaho	$ 1,053
23	Kentucky	$ 1,503	49	New Hampshire	$ 983
24	Washington	$ 1,499	50	Maine	$ 964
25	Pennsylvania	$ 1,440	51	Ohio	$ 926

Source: http://www.insure.com/car-insurance/car-insurance-rates.html

PREMIUM BEHAVIOR

Some insurance companies offer discounts for certain types of behavior. If, for example, you pay your premium all at once instead of monthly, you might receive a small discount. Other potential discount-worthy behavior includes:

- Getting good grades

- Taking a defensive driving course

- Having a car alarm

- Purchasing multiple policies, such as home or auto insurance, from the same company

- Allowing a car insurance company to record your behind-the-wheel behavior with a small device. Good behavior means a lower premium. This is called usage-based insurance.

Have you ever bought a TV, smartphone, or computer and had the salesperson lean in to share unsettling stories about the odds of your new gadget's breaking? Why would they do that? So they can explain that for a small fee, you'll be protected—either in the form of a new item or a free repair—if your new item goes kaput.

They're attempting to sell you a warranty. Typically, a warranty promises that if something goes wrong with an item because of a defect, the item will be repaired or replaced at no cost. A warranty is essentially a type of insurance—it's an agreement from the manufacturer that the customer will be compensated for problems in certain circumstances.

Most consumer purchases include a manufacturer's warranty for a certain period of time, such as 90 days to a year. Cars usually have warranties for a period of time or a certain number of miles, whichever comes first.

Warranties don't cover everything. They don't go into effect if the problem is your fault or if it results from general wear and tear. For example, if you get in a fight with your brother and throw the remote through the new TV, a warranty wouldn't cover the damage. And if you've had the TV for 15 years and the picture starts to look fuzzy, chances are a manufacturer won't replace it. But if the picture on your brand-new TV isn't clear and sharp, the company will either offer to repair it or give you a new TV.

EXTENDED WARRANTIES

Basic warranties that come with products are free. But it's typical for a salesperson to try to sell you additional protection, especially on expensive items. These plans are called extended warranties.

In general, consumer experts say extended warranties don't make much sense. Often an extended warranty costs too much, duplicates the coverage that comes with the manufacturer's warranty, or fails to cover what is most likely to break. Instead of buying an extended warranty, consider setting aside the cost of the warranty in a savings account. That way you can replace or repair the item yourself. If it doesn't break, you have extra cash in the bank.

Like all money decisions, emotion can play a role in deciding whether to purchase an additional warranty. If a warranty gives you peace of mind, then it's OK to buy one. Just be sure to understand what's covered by reading the fine print.

FACT: If you buy an extended warranty and change your mind, you may be entitled to a partial or full refund within a certain period of time. Read the fine print to learn if your extended warranty has this feature.

CHAPTER TWELVE PROTECTING YOURSELF

You've learned how to use insurance to protect some of your most important assets—your car, smartphone, and furniture. But there is one asset that cannot be replaced: YOU. Your ability to work. Your identity. Your life.

There are some tools for protection that may not even register on your radar screen. You probably figure that you're just a teen and life isn't complicated enough to have a will or life insurance. Let's see if that assumption is correct.

A will is a legal document that sets up what you'd like to happen to your property when you die. While most teens' financial lives are pretty uncomplicated, a will is a good idea if you feel strongly about which of your siblings would get your dirt bike or jewelry, or if you have a beloved pet that would need a new home. If you do have assets, either from saving or by inheriting money or property from a relative, having a will is even more important. A will is an absolute must if you have a partner or children. A will establishes guardianship—who will take care of your child if you die. You don't want to leave that decision up to the court system.

You can use legal websites or computer software to create a simple will. If you'd rather get professional help, start with your parents' or guardians' lawyer, if they have one. Some law firms also do free legal work for certain groups, including teens. Legal aid groups, which are made up of lawyers who volunteer their time to help low-income people with legal problems, are another option.

LIFE INSURANCE POLICY

Terms used in this Policy

following describe your rights and obligations under this Policy.

us, our and the Company mean Life Insurance Company.

and your means the Policy Owner named in the Policy Schedule.

inistrative rules means the rules and procedures we establish to facilitate the ___ ___ive rules ___ill amend our administrative rules from time to time. Any changes we make to ___

r any guarantee or benefit provided by this Policy.

ained Age means a Life Insured's Insurance Age plus the number of ___ from th___ licy Date to the

licy Anniversary.

eneficiary means the person or entity entitled to receive the Death Benefit when th___ esignated Life

lass means a grouping of individuals satisfying underwriting criteria related to specified aspects of h___

___bacco usage, family history and other personal history. Based on these criteria, a Life Insured can ___

___ either a Smoker or a Non-Smoker, and in either a Preferred or Standard Class. We determine th___

___ ___plicable to each Life Insured and use it to establish his or her Premium. It is specified in the Poli___

___. When your insurance ends

___ ___ under this Policy ends on the earliest of the following dates.

___ ___ the Designated Life Insured dies.

___ ___ Policy takes effect under the Exchange Privilege, as described in ___

___ ___ takes effect under the Conversion Privilege, as described in the Prov___

DO I NEED ... LIFE INSURANCE?

If you're an average teen, the answer is no. Life insurance is designed to provide financially for your loved ones when you die. It's typically used to replace the income earned by the person who died and to cover large expenses such as the cost of college for the person's children.

Teens typically don't have children or large incomes to replace. If you do work and have a family, you might consider a term life insurance policy. It covers the policyholder for a certain period of time, such as 10, 20, or 30 years, rather than the policyholder's entire life. If the policyholder dies during the time the policy is in effect—the term—the beneficiaries receive a payout. Term insurance premiums are generally lower than whole life insurance premiums.

If you don't have a family to support, there are better places to put your money. The only caution is that term life insurance policies tend to cost less the younger and healthier you are. But waiting until you're in your 20s or 30s won't mean a drastic increase in the premium.

Insurance salespeople may try to sell you a policy that has cash value as a way to protect your family and as an investment. Don't bite. These policies are expensive, and it can be tough to find room in your budget for the monthly premiums. There are better tools for investing in your future. Plus many employers offer a term life insurance policy worth one to two times your annual salary as an employee benefit. That may be enough.

Disability insurance replaces a portion of your income if you can't work for a few weeks because of a temporary condition, or if you have a chronic illness that keeps you from earning money for a long period of time. Sometimes disability insurance is included as an employee benefit. Your employer may pay for part or all of a policy or offer it as a benefit you can pay for yourself. Insurance agents also sell disability insurance policies.

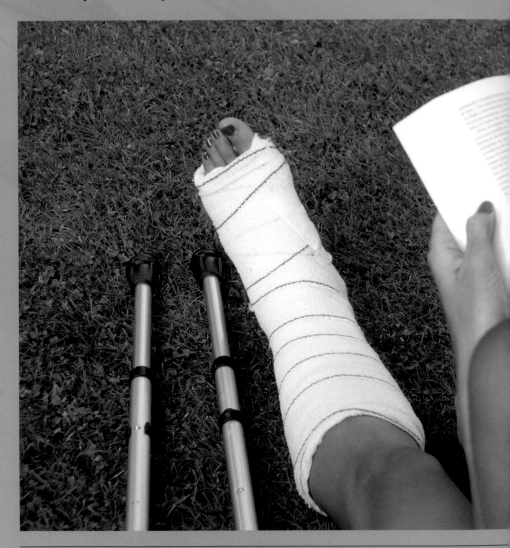

According to a survey by Learnvest, an online personal finance company, and Guardian Life Insurance Company, just 35 percent of 20- and 30-somethings have disability insurance of any kind. Most report that they don't know anyone who has become disabled or they don't think they need it for the kind of work that they do.

You might agree with the young adults who responded to the survey. You are young and healthy and don't need to scrape together money in your budget to buy insurance that covers you in the rare case that you become disabled. But it's more common for a young person to become disabled than you think. The U.S. Social Security Administration says that one in four of today's 20-year-olds will become disabled sometime during their careers.

Social Security offers disability insurance to workers who have paid into the system. But that usually isn't an adequate amount of coverage for workers and doesn't help in the event of a shorter-term illness or injury.

PROTECTING YOUR IDENTITY

Someone's identity is stolen every three seconds, according to research company Javelin Strategy and Research. This amounts to 12 million identity fraud victims in the United States a year.

Young people are attractive targets for thieves because they are looking for clean identities—people with few, if any, blemishes on their credit reports. A credit report is a record of your financial accounts. Financial institutions and others consult it to decide whether to lend you money, accept your credit card application, or rent you an apartment.

Have you ever shared a computer password or PIN with a friend? Or recycled bank account documents without shredding them? These actions may seem harmless enough. Your friend isn't going to do anything to hurt you. And who is going to dig through your recycling bin? But both are actions that can lead to identity theft.

Identity theft occurs when someone uses your personal information for his or her benefit. It could mean someone else using your Social Security number to apply for a job or opening a credit card account in your name. Getting personal information that can be used to steal your identity is easier than you think. Personal information could be stolen onlne, from your trash or recycling bin, or from forms you might have on file at school or a doctor's office.

If your identity is stolen, it can take dozens of hours and a lot of hard work to clean up the mess. So how can you protect yourself from this crime? Nothing is foolproof, but following some simple precautions can greatly reduce your chance of becoming an identity theft victim.

- *Be careful about sharing sensitive information such as your Social Security number, your driver's license number, or your bank account number. Always ask why this information is necessary, and check with your parents or guardians if you have any doubt—even if it's a friend who is asking.*

- *Keep important documents safe. Never carry your birth certificate or Social Security card. Keep them in a locked safe at home or in a safe-deposit box at a bank.*

- *Shred, shred, shred. Never just throw away or recycle bank account statements or other papers with important numbers in plain sight. Shredding these documents and tossing the remnants in multiple recycling bins or garbage cans can thwart criminals.*

- *Check over your bank and credit card statements carefully. If someone else is using your account or credit card, you'll notice charges you don't recognize.*

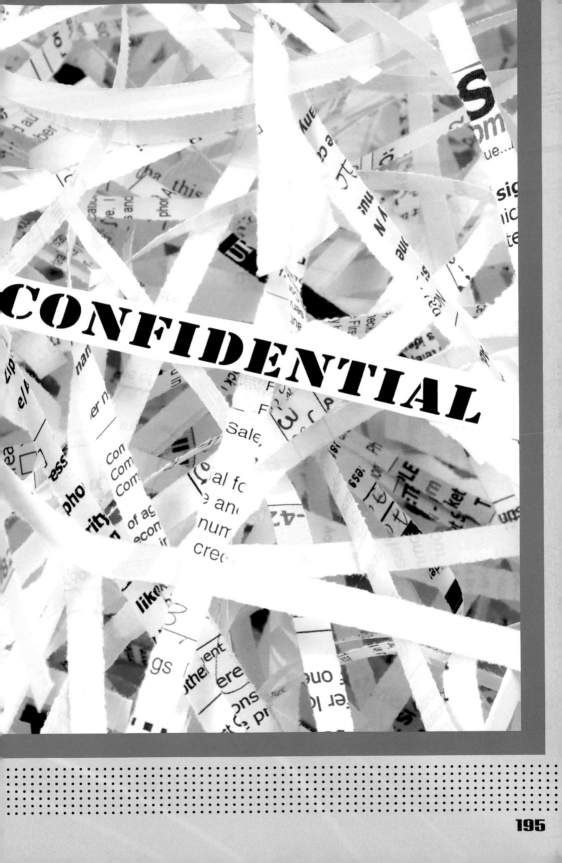

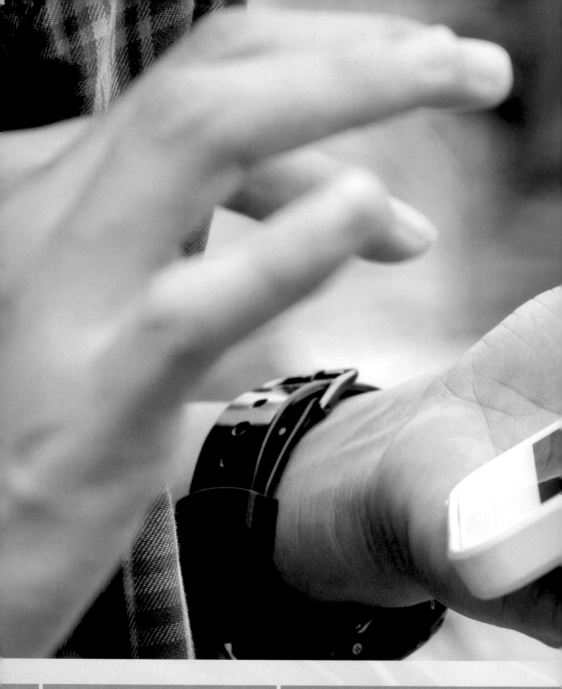

SIMPLE PRECAUTIONS

- Lock 'em up. Use the passcode function on your phone and the password feature on your laptop to protect your devices.

- Smartphones are a prime target for identity theft. You can reduce your risk by updating your operating system whenever the manufacturer makes an update available.

- Don't overshare. Keep personal info you share online to a minimum. For example, don't put your birth year, school, or middle name on your social media profiles. Also don't share any information online, such as your pet's name or grandparent's first name, that you may use as an answer for a security question that helps verify your identity at a website.

- Check your credit report. Every year you are entitled to a free credit report from each of the three major credit bureaus from the website www.annualcreditreport.com. Access your report only through this official site. Other sites advertise free credit reports but often require other purchases to unlock your report. Steer clear. If you request one credit report every four months, it's a good way to monitor whether your identity has been stolen without having to pay for an identity theft monitoring service.

WHAT TO DO

Identity thieves can thwart even the most careful consumer. If you discover that your identity has been stolen, immediately take these steps to prevent further damage:

FRAUD ALERT

Place a fraud alert on your credit report. Find the number to call of one of the major credit reporting agencies—Equifax, Experian, or TransUnion—on their website.

FILE REPORT

File a police report.

CLOSE ACCOUNTS

Close any compromised accounts and dispute any charges that you didn't incur by contacting your credit card company, which will open up an investigation.

LODGE COMPLAINT

File a complaint with the Federal Trade Commission at https://www.ftccomplaintassistant.gov and create an identity theft report. It can be used to fight fraudulent charges and any other fallout from your stolen identity.

Experts suggest a different password for every account to avoid problems in case one of them experiences a security breach. Having to remember dozens of complex passwords is tough, especially since writing them down carries its own risks. But you don't want to be the chump who uses "password," "123456," or another easy-to-guess and all-too-common password to access your bank account.

Wondering how to create foolproof passwords that you can remember? Here are some suggestions:

Make it eight: Make your password at least eight characters long. A sentence might be easier to remember than a combination of random characters.

Mix it up: Create a password that includes several uppercase and lowercase letters, numbers, symbols, and punctuation marks.

Change it up: Don't keep the same passwords forever. Yes, it's a hassle to switch them, and most accounts don't require password resets. But experts recommend you set a reminder every three months to change your passwords.

After following these tips, if you still wonder how your password stacks up, run it through an online password checker, such as Microsoft Safety and Security Center, https://www.microsoft.com/security/pc-security/password-checker.aspx.

TIME IS MONEY

Resolving identity theft issues is time-consuming. According to Javelin Strategy and Research, identity theft victims spend about 58 hours trying to repair damage to their existing accounts and 165 hours fixing the damage caused by new accounts fraudulently opened in their names. That's the equivalent of more than five 40-hour workweeks!

GLOSSARY

401(k)—retirement account offered by an employer that provides tax incentives for using it

annual percentage rate (APR)—yearly interest rate charged on outstanding credit card balances

asset—item of value, such as money or property

bachelor's degree—a degree from a college or university, usually completed in four years

behavioral economics—branch of economics that uses psychology to explain why and how people make financial decisions

bond—certificate issued by a corporation or government to raise money; the issuer pays interest on the bond to the lender for a certain amount of time and then returns the principal to the lender

budget—plan for spending and saving money

capital—amount of money needed to start a business or complete a project

claim—request for payment of a loss covered by an insurance policy

commission—payment based on a percentage of sales; also fee paid to an agent or employee for transacting a piece of business or performing a service

consumer—someone who buys and uses goods and services

co-signer—person who takes on a joint obligation to pay back a debt; parents may be required to co-sign on loans to teens

credit score—number generated by a statistical model that is used to help financial institutions to decide whether to lend a consumer money; the higher the score, the better

credit union—a not-for-profit financial institution set up by members of a group

deductible—amount of money an insured person pays before an insurance company pays for the remainder of the cost

diversification—concept of putting money into various types of investments, such as stocks, bonds, cash, and real estate

down payment—money paid up front when making a major purchase involving borrowing; the down payment is typically calculated as a percentage of the total cost of the item

entrepreneur—person who starts a business or company

escrow account—account, typically related to a home mortgage, where money is kept by a third person until it's time to pay insurance or other expenses

fixed expense—an expense that stays basically the same from month to month, such as rent and car payments

freelance—to work for multiple companies, usually with a contract that lasts a certain amount of time or on a per-project basis

frugal—careful in spending and using resources

grace period—time a borrower is allowed after a payment is due to make the payment without additional interest being owed

gross pay—total amount of money earned before taxes and benefit costs are deducted

identity theft—stealing another person's identification and other personal information for financial gain

index—an imaginary portfolio of securities representing a particular market; stock and bond indexes are used to construct index mutual funds

inertia—law of physics stating that a body at rest remains at rest unless acted on by an external force

inflation—an economic state in which prices of goods and services continue to rise

insurance score—rating computed and used by insurance companies that represents the probability that an insured person will file an insurance claim during his or her coverage

interest—fee charged to borrow money; generally, interest is calculated as a percentage of the amount borrowed or lent

internship—work a person does for little or no money in order to gain experience

liability—something that is owed, such as loans and credit card debt

median—middle; half of workers make more than the median income and half of workers make less

mutual fund—savings tool that pools money from multiple investors for the purpose of buying a variety of investments

negotiate—to bargain or discuss something in order to come to an agreement

networking—contacting other people in the same industry in order to find a job

net worth—value of what you own after subtracting liabilities from assets

opportunity cost—next best alternative that is given up when a choice is made; for example, when you spend your money, you lose your "opportunity" to use it in other ways

policy—written agreement for insurance between an insurance company and a person who has insurance

premium—amount paid for insurance

principal—original amount invested or the amount borrowed or still owed on a loan, separate from interest

quote—amount of money that an insurance company calculates as the cost of providing insurance

recession—temporary slowing of business activity

résumé—document that lists an employee's education, work experience, and skills

return—amount of money earned on a particular investment, typically represented as a percentage

risk tolerance—amount of risk a person is willing to handle

salary—fixed amount of earnings per pay period

stock—value of a company, divided into shares when sold to investors

time horizon—length of time of an investment; time horizon can range from days to years

variable expense—an expense that varies from month to month, such as food or clothing expenses

warranty—written statement that promises the good condition of a product and states that the maker is responsible for repairing or replacing the product, usually for a certain period of time after its purchase

Bankrate. 6 May 2014.
http://www.bankrate.com

Benefitspro. 2 May 2014.
http://www.benefitspro.com

Bestprep. 1 May 2014. http://bestprep.org

Brookings. Quality. Independence. Impact.
1 May 2014. http://www.brookings.edu

Car Insurance Rates by State. Insure.com. 2 May
2014. http://www.insure.com/car-insurance/
car-insurance-rates.html

Charities Review Council. 6 May 2014.
http://www.smartgivers.org

Charity Navigator. 6 May 2014.
http://www.charitynavigator.org

Choose to Save. 7 May 2014.
http://www.choosetosave.org

The College Board. 6 May 2014.
https://www.collegeboard.org

The College Payoff. Georgetown University's
Center on Education and the Workforce. 5 Aug.
2011. 1 May 2014. http://cew.georgetown.edu/
collegepayoff

Consumer Financial Protection Bureau. 7 May
2014. http://www.consumerfinance.gov

Consumers Union. 2 May 2014.
http://consumersunion.org

Credit Union National Association.
7 May 2014. http://www.cuna.org

Demystifying the Insurance Industry: The Truth
About Insurance. 2 May 2014. http://www.
thetruthaboutinsurance.com

Disability Planner: Social Security Protection If
You Become Disabled. 2 May 2014.
http://www.ssa.gov/dibplan/

Employment Policies Institute. 1 May 2014.
http://www.epionline.org

Farrell, Chris. The New Frugality.
New York: Bloomsbury Press, 2010.

Federal Student Aid. 6 May 2014.
https://fafsa.ed.gov

Federal Trade Commission: Protecting America's
Consumers. 2 May 2014. http://www.ftc.gov

Finaid! 7 May 2014. http://www.finaid.org

Financial Industry Regulatory Authority.
7 May 2014. http://www.finra.org

Foreign Policy Association.
7 May 2014. http://www.fpa.org

Franklin Institute. 7 May 2014.
https://www.fi.edu

Guidestar. 6 May 2014.
http://www.guidestar.org

HealthCare.gov. 2 May 2014.
https://www.healthcare.gov

High School Financial Planning Program.
2 May 2014. http://www.hsfpp.org

Identity Theft Resource Center. 2 May 2014.
http://www.idtheftcenter.org

Insurance Information Institute.
2 May 2014. http://www.iii.org

Internal Revenue Service. 1 May 2014.
http://www.irs.gov

The Internet Guide to Funding College and
Section 529 Savings Plans. 7 May 2014.
http://www.savingforcollege.com/

Iseek. Minnesota's Career, Education, and Job
Resource. 1 May 2014. http://www.iseek.org

Job Search, Interview & Employment Advice.
1 May 2014. http://jobsearch.about.com

Jump Start. Financial Smarts for Students.
1 May 2014. http://jumpstart.org

Lewis, Casey. "What to Wear to a Job Interview."
Teen Vogue. 9 May 2014. http://www.teenvogue.
com/fashion/what-to-wear/2012-05/job-
interview/?slide=1

Mapping Your Future. 6 May 2014.
http://www.mappingyourfuture.org

The Mint: Fun Financial Literacy Activities for
Kids, Teens, Parents and Teachers. 1 May 2014.
http://www.themint.org

National Assoc. of Insurance Commissioners. 2 May 2014. http://www.naic.org

National Center for Education Statistics. 6 May 2014. http://nces.ed.gov

National Crime Prevention Council. 2 May 2014. http://www.ncpc.org

National Endowment for Financial Education. 7 May 2014. www.nefe.org

Projectionstudentdebt.org. 6 May 2014. http://www.projectionstudentdebt.org

Robin, Vicki, and Joe Dominguez. *Your Money or Your Life: 9 Steps to Transforming Your Relationship with Money and Achieving Financial Independence*. New York: Penguin Books, 2008.

Schwab Moneywise. 6 May 2014. http://www.schwabmoneywise.com/public/moneywise/home

Share Save Spend. Money + Meaning. 1 May 2014. http://www.sharesavespend.com

Tobias, Andrew P. *The Only Investment Guide You'll Ever Need*. Boston: Mariner Books/Houghton Mifflin Harcourt, 2010.

United States Department of Labor. 7 May 2014. http://www.dol.gov

Wall Street Survivor. 8 May 2014. http://www.wallstreetsurvivor.com

What's My Score. 6 May 2014. http://whatsmyscore.org

Yahoo! Finance. 3 June 2014. http://finance.yahoo.com

SOURCE NOTES

Page 9, line 1: Notorious B.I.G. lyrics: "Mo Money Mo Problems." 9 May 2014. http://www.azlyrics.com/lyrics/notoriousbig/momoneymoproblems.html

Page 9, line 3: Hank Williams Jr. lyrics: "Money Can't Buy Happiness." 9 May 2014. http://www.sweetslyrics.com/255474.Hank%20Williams%20Jr.%20-%20Money%20Can't%20Buy%20Happiness.html

Page 29, line 1: Teen Business Link. "Ideas for Your Business." U.S. Small Business Administration. 9 May 2014. http://archive.sba.gov/teens/ideas.html

Page 30, line 12: Teen Business Link. "Put It in Writing." U.S. Small Business Administration. 9 May 2014. http://archive.sba.gov/teens/myplan.html

Page 35, line 1: E-mail interview. 30 May 2013.

Page 36, line 4: Phone interview. 5 June 2013.

Page 37, line 17: Peggy Gibbs. "Key Skills for Youth to Succeed and Thrive." Camp BizSmart. 16 May 2013. 9 May 2014. http://campbizsmart.org/2013/05/16/key-skills-for-youth-to-succeed-and-thrive/

Page 53, line 2: Women Don't Ask: Negotiation and the Gender Divide. 9 May 2014. http://www.womendontask.com/stats.html

Page 76: E-mail interview. 21 Aug. 2013.

Page 80: Benjamin Franklin. *The Way to Wealth*. 9 May 2014. http://www.bartleby.com/400/prose/351.html

Page 117, line 23: Jesse Singal. "Daniel Kahneman's Gripe with Behavioral Economics." *The Daily Beast*. 26 April 2013. 5 May 2014. http://www.thedailybeast.com/articles/2013/04/26/daniel-kahneman-s-gripe-with-behavioral-economics.html

Page 133, line 8: Natasha Chandel. "Macklemore 'Pops Some Tags' While Thrift Shopping." MTV. 20 Dec. 2012. 5 May 2014. http://www.mtv.com/news/1699304/macklemore-thrift-shop/

Page 147, line 1: Trends in Higher Education. 14 May 2014. https://trends.collegeboard.org/college-pricing/figures-tables/average-published-undergraduate-charges-sector-2013-14

Page 153, line 9: Christina Couch. "How much college debt is too much?" Bankrate.com. 5 May 2014. http://www.bankrate.com/finance/college-finance/how-much-college-debt-is-too-much-1.aspx

Page 155, line 1: Phone and e-mail interviews. 7 Aug. 2013.

INDEX